# Usborne
# Stories
## from
# Shakespeare

Illustrated by
## Elena Temporin
Retold by Anna Claybourne
Designed by Laura Fearn

SCHOLASTIC INC.
New York  Toronto  London  Auckland  Sydney
Mexico City  New Delhi  Hong Kong  Buenos Aires

Usborne

# Stories
## from
# Shakespeare

Edited by Jane Chisholm

Additional design by Nickey Butler

Digital manipulation by John Russell

ISBN 0-439-88984-7

12 11 10 9 8 7 6 5 4 3 2 1        6 7 8 9 10 11/0
Printed in the U.S.A.                    40
First Scholastic printing, October 2006

# Contents

# Twelfth Night

"If music be the food of love, play on!" declared Duke Orsino of Illyria, reclining on a pile of silken pillows in his plush palace. The musicians began to play again. But however hard they tried, they couldn't make Orsino happy.

"Oh, Olivia!" he groaned. "Why don't you love me? I'm desperate! What can I do?"

Just then, Orsino's servant Valentine came in, wearing his outdoor cloak and boots.

"Valentine, my good man," Orsino cried. "How is Olivia today? What did she say to my message? And did she like the flowers? Come on, tell me everything!"

"I'm sorry, my lord," said Valentine anxiously. "I didn't even set eyes on her ladyship. Her maid took the flowers at the door. She says Olivia refuses to see any men at all – she's still in mourning for her dead brother."

"Still!?" shouted Orsino. "But then," he added more thoughtfully, "if she loved a mere brother so much, think how much she'll love me, when she finally sees sense!"

～

Not far away, where the waves of the Adriatic Sea crashed onto Illyria's sandy white beaches, the survivors of a terrible shipwreck had just dragged themselves to safety. It looked as if only the captain, three of his crew, and one of their passengers, a young lady named Viola, had made it ashore.

"W-what is this place?" gasped Viola, soaking and shivering.

"It's my homeland, madam – Illyria," said the captain. "I thank the gods we are safe."

Viola felt for her purse. It was still there, full of gold pieces, where she had tied it securely at her waist. But something else was missing – something much more important.

"My brother!" cried Viola, looking around in a panic. "I thought he was with us! Where is my twin brother, Sebastian?"

"I saw him clinging to the mast, my lady," the captain reassured her, "and that was surely the wisest thing to do, as it must float to shore somewhere."

"Aye, your brother's a strong lad," said another sailor kindly.

Viola felt tears pricking her eyes. "Who rules this kingdom?" she asked.

"The noble duke, Orsino," replied the sea captain. "A kind and virtuous gentleman – although somewhat foolish in his love for Countess Olivia."

"And who's she?"

"A beautiful countess," the captain said, "but since her father died, and her brother too, she's shut herself away in her house, and won't let any man woo her."

"Oh...!" said Viola. "If only I could work for her, and be her lady-in-waiting! Her house would be a safe place to stay while I wait to see if my brother has survived."

"Ah, now that won't be so easy," said the sailor, "for she'll not hear of any visitors."

"Then perhaps I could work for the duke instead," said Viola. She turned to the captain. "Will you help me, sir? If you can find me some clothes, I'll disguise myself as a boy. You can take me to Orsino and tell him I'd make a good servant – and he might take me on as a page."

"I'll do as you ask, madam," the captain replied. "Your secret's safe with us."

Meanwhile, in Olivia's house, Maria, the maid, was bustling down the hall. The huge bunch of flowers she was carrying blocked her view, and she tripped over a pair of outstretched feet. They belonged to Sir Toby Belch, Olivia's uncle, who was asleep on the kitchen steps.

"Sir Toby, what are you doing there!?" Maria scolded. "You look as if you've been up all night! You were drinking, weren't you, with that scoundrel Sir Andrew? Heavens above, it's no wonder my lady's had enough of men, when all she ever sees is you two!"

"I'll have you know," said Sir Toby, sitting up, "Sir Andrew Aguecheek is a perfect gentleman. He's not just here for fun, you know – he intends to propose to my niece."

"Oh, what nonsense!" laughed Maria, and she hurried away. Just then, Sir Andrew, who was old, fat and not very handsome, came stumbling along the hall.

"Ah, Sir Andrew," Sir Toby yawned. "Time for breakfast?"

"Why not?" replied Sir Andrew; and they set off to find something to eat.

~~

A few days later, Viola found herself a job as a page at Orsino's palace. The captain and his wife had given her a pile of clothes their sons had grown out of and with her hair tucked under her cap, she easily passed for a handsome young lad.

"It's amazing, Cesario," said Valentine – for "Cesario" was the false name Viola had chosen. "The duke's been in a terrible mood for months, but he's completely cheered up since you arrived! How do you do it?"

Before she could answer, Orsino appeared. "Ah, Cesario," he said, "just the person I was looking for!" He frowned impatiently at Valentine, who scurried away.

"Now then, Cesario. I've told you all about my love for Countess Olivia. I'd like you to call on her today, on my behalf."

"But... won't I be turned away, like the others?" asked Viola, trying to make her voice sound as deep as possible.

"If you are, don't stand for it!" said Orsino. "Wait at the gate – *insist* on seeing her!"

"And if I succeed?"

"Then tell her everything – how I adore her, how I swoon with longing for her all day long, and can barely leave my bed for lovesickness!" Orsino cried, dramatically. "It will sound so much better coming from you, than from any of my other servants."

"I don't see why," said Viola, feeling confused. She hadn't expected any of this. She had hoped to be given simple things to do, like carrying parcels or helping in the pantry.

"Because you're so young, she won't feel threatened," Orsino explained. "Why, you've hardly a hair on your chin, and your voice is like a woman's. Olivia's sure to like you!"

Viola looked up at the duke uncomfortably. Had he guessed her secret? She wasn't sure. "I'll do my best, my lord," she said at last. But, as she left the palace and set off along the short road into the city, Viola realized that something else was bothering her.

It was Orsino. His kindness, and his friendly laugh, and his beautiful brown eyes. Whenever she was with him, she felt happy. Viola knew what was happening. She was falling in love with him herself.

~⁓~

Maria was busy dusting the silverware when she spotted Feste, Olivia's jester.

"Feste!" she called. "Where have you been? My lady needs cheering up. It's time she stopped mourning and found herself a husband – and I don't mean Sir Andrew Aguecheek! Can't you persuade her?"

"Well, here she comes," said Feste. "I'll see what I can do."

Olivia's heavy mourning clothes rustled as she stepped down the grand staircase, flanked by her ladies-in-waiting, her pageboys, and her miserable-faced old butler, Malvolio. Maria looked at her and sighed. She was truly beautiful, with her golden hair and her cherry-red lips. Yet the sadness in her eyes made Maria want to cry. Olivia's lovely face was being wasted – kept indoors all day, and never allowed to laugh in the sun.

"Take the fool away," Olivia said when she saw Feste. "I do not wish to be amused."

"You heard!" Feste told the other servants. "Take my lady away!"

"How dare you!" snapped Malvolio. "You are the fool, not she!"

"That's enough," said Olivia. "We'll have no more fooling."

"But wait!" said Feste. "You *are* the fool, my lady, and I can prove it!"

"Very well," said Olivia patiently, with just a hint of a smile. "Prove it."

"I shall," Feste grinned. "Why do you mourn, my lady?"

"For the death of my dear brother."

"Indeed, he has probably gone to Hell, my lady."

"No indeed! My brother is in Heaven!"

"Then there is nothing to be sad about, and you are the fool!" Feste cried, doing a little dance of triumph. Olivia smiled properly this time, and found him a gold coin.

"My lady, how can you tolerate the antics of this obnoxious clown!?" demanded Malvolio angrily; but Olivia ignored him.

Just then, a footman came in. "There is another messenger from Duke Orsino, madam," he said. "I told him you were not receiving visitors, but he refuses to leave."

Olivia looked thoughtful. "Perhaps it is time I stopped mourning, after all," she said. "What is this messenger like?"

"No more than a boy, madam – with a sweet voice, and an eager face. I'm sure he's harmless."

"Show him in," said Olivia. "Maria, I will wear my veil." Maria hurried to fetch the veil as the gates were unlocked, and the visitor was shown through.

Viola (disguised as Cesario, of course) stepped into the room. "Where is the lady of the house?" she asked.

"I will answer for her," said Olivia, from behind her veil.

"But are you really Countess Olivia?" asked Viola. "My speech is carefully prepared, and I don't wish to throw it away on the wrong person."

This made Olivia laugh. "Are you a jester too?" she asked.

"No, my lady, although I can truthfully say that I am not what I seem. My name is Cesario."

"I will hear your message in private," Olivia announced. She was fascinated by this polite, witty boy – so unlike most of Orsino's servants.

"Leave us alone," she said to the other servants. After they had all gone away, Olivia finally lifted her veil, and when Viola saw how beautiful she was, she forgot her speech altogether.

"My lady," she gasped. "You must not hide this beauty away. You know my master Orsino loves you, and would marry you tomorrow."

"I know his love is true," said Olivia sadly, "but unfortunately, I do not love him."

"If I were Orsino, I would not understand why."

"Love is love," said Olivia. "We cannot choose who we love. Go back to your master, and tell him I do not wish to hear from him again. Unless – "

"Yes, my lady?"

"Unless you would like to come back, and tell me how he takes the news."

～～

Meanwhile, Viola's twin brother Sebastian had arrived in Illyria. He had not drowned in the shipwreck. After a miserable day spent clinging to the floating wreckage, he had been rescued from the sea by a trading ship, and its captain, Antonio, had brought him ashore.

"Thank you so much, Antonio, for all your help," said Sebastian, shaking hands with the captain. "Now I'm here. I'll visit Duke Orsino, and tell him who I am. My father was the Marquis of Messaline – Orsino must have heard of him."

"Then it's best you don't mention me," said Antonio. "I'd rather avoid the duke."

"Why's that?" asked Sebastian.

"Well," mumbled Antonio, "the truth is, I used to be a pirate. It was a long time ago, but I'm still wanted in Illyria for crimes at sea. If Orsino finds out I'm here, I'll be arrested."

"But you saved my life!" said Sebastian. "Surely you'll be forgiven? And since I owe my life to you, I'll help you in any way I can."

"Well," said Antonio, "there is one thing you could do for me. Could I give you my purse to carry? I'm afraid my old enemies will rob me for my gold. I could leave it with you until I'm ready to set sail again."

"Of course," said Sebastian, taking the purse. "We'll meet here again tomorrow."

Sebastian set off inland. He thanked the heavens that he had been saved, but his heart ached, for he was sure his twin sister Viola had drowned. The twins had been best friends all their lives, and everyone always said how alike they looked. Now, although he knew he was lucky to be alive, Sebastian almost wished he could have left the world with his sister, just as he had come into the world with her.

～✌

That night, Sir Toby and Sir Andrew were up late again. They sat in Olivia's kitchen, eating leftovers, drinking wine and talking nonsense, until Feste came into the room.

"Aha, a clown!" Sir Andrew cried. "Just what we need! Sing us a song, clown!"

"I will, for sixpence," said Feste. Toby gave him a coin, and Feste began to sing:

*What is love? 'Tis not hereafter,*
*Present mirth hath present laughter;*
*What's to come is still unsure.*
*In delay there lies no plenty,*
*Then come kiss me sweet and twenty:*
*Youth's a stuff will not endure.*

"Maria!" Sir Toby shouted. "Bring us some more wine!"

"Alright, I'm coming!" Maria came in from the pantry with a large jug. "But keep the noise down! My lady's in a very odd mood today, after that visit from Orsino's page."

"Ah, she's probably just pining for me!" said Sir Andrew, and they all burst out laughing. Maria filled all their glasses with wine, and poured a small one for herself. They were all having so much fun, they didn't hear Malvolio's footsteps on the stairs.

"Enough of this racket!" he shrieked, making them all jump. "How can my poor lady Olivia be expected to get any sleep at all! As for you, Maria – what were you thinking? Giving these louts and layabouts more wine, when they've certainly had enough! Well, my lady shall be hearing about this – I'll make sure of it!" And he marched back upstairs.

"Pompous old fool!" grumbled Maria. "I've a mind to play a proper trick on him."

"What? Tell us!" They all leaned forward around the table.

"Well," Maria whispered, "you know you and the duke are not alone, Sir Andrew, in hoping to win my lady's hand in marriage. Our bossy butler fancies himself the perfect husband for her. And I'm going to write him a love letter, in her handwriting."

"He'll think she loves him!" exclaimed Sir Andrew, grinning with glee.

"He'll make such a fool of himself!" Sir Toby squealed.

"Shhh now," said Maria, "I'm going to bed. And in the morning, I'll get my revenge on that interfering old idiot. Just you wait and see."

❧

The next day, Duke Orsino called for his best servant – his new page, Cesario. "Come and sit here with me, Cesario," Orsino said, "and we'll talk about love."

"Very well," said Viola, trying to stop herself from trembling with passion for him.

"I have to talk to someone," Orsino confessed. "I'm so in love with Olivia, I can hardly bear it. I can tell you know about being in love, don't you? You know how I feel."

"Yes I do, my lord. But Olivia cannot love you. She has said so."

Orsino shrugged. "And who is it that you love, Cesario? What's she like?"

"Well, she looks a little like you. I mean, she has the same complexion."

"Really? And how old is she?"

"Erm... about your age."

"Well, you take care, Cesario. Women don't feel love as strongly as we men do, you know. Certainly, no one could love me as much as I love Olivia."

"I don't think that's true, sir," said Viola.

"Why not?" asked Orsino, looking into her eyes. "How do you know?"

"M-my father's daughter," Viola stammered, "was in love with a man, and I'm sure no man could have felt more love than she did."

"And what happened to this – erm – sister of yours?"

12

"She kept her love a secret," Viola said, "and suffered it for a long time."

"Indeed?" mused Orsino, smiling at her, so that she thought she would faint with longing for him. "And I suppose she pined away and died of sorrow?"

"As far as I know, I am now my father's only child," said Viola, truthfully, but her face burned with embarrassment. "Shall I – would you like me to visit Olivia again for you?"

"Why not?" Orsino agreed, and Viola hurried out of the palace. She wondered again – had Orsino guessed she was a woman in disguise? She couldn't tell.

∾

In Olivia's garden, Maria, Sir Toby and Sir Andrew were hiding behind a bushy box tree. A letter, carefully written by Maria that morning, and folded and stamped with Olivia's seal, lay on a stone bench by the garden wall, and Malvolio was coming along the path.

"Oh, my lady," Malvolio sighed to himself. "Oh, to be your husband!"

"He's thinking about it already, and he hasn't even seen the letter!" hissed Sir Toby.

"Ah, how grand I would look in a velvet gown!" Malvolio dreamed aloud. "Rising late, and dining with Olivia! Oh! What's this?" he cried, spying the letter. He picked it up.

"'To my unknown beloved,'" he read. "It is Olivia's seal! But who can it be for?" And he ripped it open – for whether it was for him, or for someone else, the nosy old butler considered the letter to be his business. He read the letter aloud:

*My dearest beloved,*

*Everyone knows I am in love – but who with? The answer is simple. He whom I love, is at my command. If you are reading this, my dear, do not be afraid, even though I am your lady. When we are married, you shall be my lord. To prepare yourself for this happy state, do not act like a servant. Put on airs and graces, and be smug and smiling. And always wear your yellow stockings – you know how I adore them!*

*From your loving lady*

"It is for me! It is for me!" Malvolio cried, hopping and skipping around the garden, while the three plotters behind the tree almost fell over laughing. "For she said she admired my yellow stockings – just this week, she said it! I shall go and put them on again! And I shall smile, and show airs and graces, just as she asks! My lady, I am on my way!"

For the second time in two days, Viola arrived at Olivia's house and knocked at the gates. Through them, she could see Feste sitting in the garden, playing on a lute.

"Excuse me," she called. "Are you Countess Olivia's fool?"

"Oh, no," said Feste. "She doesn't have a fool of her own – she's not married yet."

Viola laughed. "Very funny. You *are* her jester, aren't you? But that's nothing to be ashamed of. It takes wits to be a proper fool." And she gave him a gold coin.

As Feste opened the gates, Olivia came out of the house. "Cesario!" she cried. "My dearest Cesario, what brings you here?"

"You asked me to bring news of Orsino, my lady, and I do. He still loves you."

"Please, Cesario, don't tell me about him. I would much rather hear about you. You see, ever since I first saw you, I... well, I've been thinking about you all the time. I think I love you, Cesario. Will you marry me?"

"Olivia," gasped Viola, "please don't think of me like that! I could never be your husband."

"You mean you're too young!" said Olivia, "but that doesn't matter to me. You'll grow into a fine man – anyone can see that."

"Please, listen," Viola insisted. "I will never marry a woman. Do you understand?"

But Olivia didn't. Luckily, at that moment, their meeting was interrupted.

"My lady!" cried Maria, rushing into the garden, followed by Sir Andrew and Sir Toby. "Oh madam, come and see what's happened to

Malvolio. I'm sure he's gone insane! He's walking in a strange way – and he won't stop smiling!"

"He's leaping around like a clown!" added Sir Andrew.

"Malvolio? Smiling? Leaping?" Olivia got up to come indoors, but at that moment they saw Malvolio on his way down the garden path. He was wearing his yellow stockings, tied with bright red ribbons. To show them off properly, he lifted his feet high in the air with each step. As he pranced along, he grinned broadly, tilting his head from side to side.

"Malvolio? Are you alright?" Olivia asked.

"Never better, my lady!" the butler beamed. "I am doing as you asked, my darling!" Sir Toby, Sir Andrew and Maria were red-faced with suppressed laughter.

"What on earth are you talking about?" said Olivia.

"I think poor Malvolio is unwell, my lady," Maria said, pretending to be concerned.

"Malvolio," said Olivia. "you'd better go to bed. Maria is right – you're unwell."

"To bed!" cried Malvolio, grinning again. "I'll see you there, darling!"

"It really is time I was leaving," Viola tried to say, but no one was listening.

"Have him confined to his bedroom at once," Olivia whispered to Maria, "and I'll send for the doctor."

∾

Just as it seemed things could not possibly get any more confusing, they heard a commotion behind them at the half-open garden gate. A terrified-looking man, dressed in sea captain's clothes, ran into the garden from the street and rushed up to Viola.

"I thought it was you!" he said. "Thank goodness I've found you! They're after me! Orsino's men! Just give me back that purse I left with you, and I'll be able to pay them off!"

"I'm sorry," said Viola, "I don't know you. But I can lend you money, if you need it."

"It's me, Antonio!" said Antonio. "What do you mean, you don't know me? I saved you from drowning! Sebastian, it's me!"

"Sebastian...?" Viola repeated in shock. "You mean – "

Olivia stepped in. "This is Cesario," she said firmly. "Now get out of my garden."

Just then, three of Orsino's officers marched into the garden and grabbed Antonio. "Excuse us, madam," one of them said to Olivia. "This man is wanted by the duke."

As he was dragged away, Antonio called out, "Sebastian, how could you forsake me!"

"Wait!" Viola shouted. Did this mean her dear brother was alive and safe? She quickly gathered her things and set off to follow the guards back to Orsino's palace.

✺

Not long afterwards, the real Sebastian walked past Olivia's house. Feste ran to open the gates. "Cesario, you're back!" he said. "Have you changed your mind about my lady?"

"What? Who are you?" asked Sebastian.

"Aha, trying to play tricks on me!" said Feste, dragging Sebastian in by the hand. "But it won't work. I know you've decided to accept her proposal. You can't resist!"

"Cesario!" Olivia cried, rushing out of the house. "Have you changed your mind? Will you be mine? Oh, do come inside with me!"

"Well, I, erm – " Sebastian had been about to explain that this was obviously a case of mistaken identity. But this beautiful lady appeared to want to be his girlfriend, and it seemed too good a chance to miss. "Alright then," he said, and followed her in.

✺

Upstairs, Sir Toby, Sir Andrew and Maria were teasing Malvolio through the door of his locked bedroom. When Feste arrived, they persuaded him to pretend to be the doctor.

"Oh Malvolio!" he called in a silly accent. "'Tis I, Dr. Topaz!"

"There's nothing wrong with me!" groaned Malvolio. "I've been tricked! Let me out!"

"Tricked?" Feste shouted. "But I was told you were unwell! Since you can't tell the difference, I pronounce you completely insane!" The others all burst out laughing.

"You're not Dr. Topaz!" shouted Malvolio. "Who is that? Feste, is that you?"

"Oh, poor Malvolio," Maria whispered. "Perhaps he's learned his lesson now."

"Feste!" Malvolio yelled. "Bring me some paper, so I can write my lady a message!"

"Perhaps we should let him have some paper," said Maria. "We don't want to get into Olivia's bad books, after all." So Feste fetched a piece of paper, and slid it under the door. Soon the scrawled message was poked back. Feste put it in his pocket. "I'll give it to her later," he called, and they left Malvolio to suffer for just a little longer.

❧

"What can this all mean?" Sebastian asked himself, sitting in the garden in the sun, while Olivia went into town. "First I go to meet my friend Antonio, and he's not there. And I've still got his money," he remembered, checking the purse. "Then I suddenly find myself with a beautiful girlfriend! It doesn't make sense. Perhaps I'm insane, but I don't think so. Or perhaps she is – but then, how could she run this huge household?" He frowned.

"Cesario!" Olivia was back, and with her was a priest. "I do hope you won't mind us getting married so quickly. It's just – well, you seemed so reluctant before, and I don't want you changing your mind again!"

"What did you say? Married? And anyway, my name's not – "

"I know it's a little sudden, but we'll be happy, I promise!" She pulled him up by the hand. "We're just going to that church across the road – it's all arranged! Come on!"

"But – my lady, I – "

"Come on!" And with the priest in tow, she hauled Sebastian into the church.

❧

When Viola arrived at the palace, Orsino was gone. He had decided to walk into the city, and the officers, still dragging Antonio in chains, had gone to find him. Viola finally caught up with them in the square in front of Olivia's house. She was about to speak to Antonio, when the officers spotted Orsino.

"My lord," their leader shouted. "We have caught the pirate Antonio!"

"No – please don't hurt him," Viola interrrupted. "He's a good man – I'm sure of it."

"It's true," pleaded Antonio, "I've mended my ways. I rescued this lad from the sea just yesterday, and risked my life to bring him to safety in Illyria."

"That's nonsense," said Orsino. "Cesario has been working for me for several days."

"Cesario, my dear! Where have you been?" It was Olivia, stepping out of her front door, followed by her servants and attendants.

"I'm sorry, my lady," said Viola. "I'm here to speak to Orsino, not to you."

"But you're not his servant any more. You're my husband now – you're a count!"

"What?!" said Orsino, grabbing Viola by the arm. "You have married Olivia?"

"We got married this morning," said Olivia.

"How could you?" said Orsino, staring at Viola in horror. "I thought you were..."

Viola gazed back at him. "You thought I was what?"

"I have realized I don't love Olivia," Orsino told her. "You see – if my suspicions are correct – it's you I love."

"What?" cried Olivia. "Don't be silly, Orsino! Cesario's a boy! And he's my husband!"

"I thought *I* was your husband..." said a voice behind them.

"Sebastian!" Viola shouted joyfully. "You're alive!"

"Sebastian!" cried Antonio. "There you are! At last! Where's my purse?"

"Sebastian?" said Orsino and Olivia together. "Who's Sebastian?"

"My brother!" said Viola, and she pulled off her cap and let her long hair fall down. Once she had hugged Sebastian, Orsino took her in his arms. "I knew it!" he said. "I knew you were a woman! But who are you?"

"My name is Viola," Viola told him – and everyone else. "I am the daughter of the Marquis of Messaline – and the twin sister of this man, Sebastian of Messaline."

"Then, Viola," said Orsino, kneeling down, "will you be my wife?"

"I will," said Viola, her heart almost bursting with happiness.

"And are you happy to be mine?" Sebastian asked Olivia, kissing her.

"Why, Sebastian, I'm delighted," Olivia laughed.

"To celebrate my wedding," Orsino announced, "prisoners shall be freed, and rogues forgiven. Antonio, you are free to go."

"And bossy butlers shall be forgiven too!" cried Feste. He gave Olivia Malvolio's letter, and as she read how he had been tricked, she began to laugh.

"Let him out," she said at last. "Perhaps he won't be so pompous from now on. And I'll celebrate *my* wedding by inviting all of you to a party at my house!"

"It must be time for a tune!" said Feste, running to fetch his lute. And, as everyone trooped into Olivia's garden, he serenaded them with a song:

*A great while ago the world begun,*
*With a hey, ho, the wind and the rain,*
*But that's all one, our play is done,*
*And we'll strive to please you every day.*

# Macbeth

"What news of the battle?" cried Prince Malcolm, as another injured, bleeding soldier was brought into King Duncan's camp.

"Good news," panted the wounded man, as the old king emerged from his tent. "Macbeth showed those Norwegians – and that traitor Macdonald! I saw Macbeth slice him open with his sword, from the belly to the back teeth. Norway fought back, but we held firm, and the battle went our way – the King of Norway is... is asking for a truce..." The man's voice trailed off, and his eyes began to close.

"Get him to a doctor!" King Duncan ordered. Then he turned to Lord Ross. "I want Macbeth rewarded for this victory," he said. "Find him and tell him that I'm making him Thane of Cawdor, in recognition of his loyal service."

∼∽

Meanwhile, Macbeth and his friend Banquo were making their way across the mist-covered moor that lay between the battlefield and the camp.

"What a horrific day," said Macbeth. "And yet a day of happiness too."

"Yes, thank Heaven the war's over," Banquo agreed. Then he paused, staring ahead.

"What?" Macbeth peered into the mist, gripping the hilt of his sword. He thought he could see the shapes of three figures, sitting patiently on the ground – almost as if they were waiting for him.

"Who are you?" demanded Banquo. "Say something!" he shouted.

"Hail, Macbeth," replied a woman's voice. "Thane of Glamis."

"That's me," said Macbeth. "What do you want with me?"

"Hail, Macbeth," said a second voice, "Thane of Cawdor."

"Hail, Macbeth," came an older voice as, through the mist, the shapes of three women, dressed in black cloaks, became clear. "Hail Macbeth, that shall be king hereafter."

"What do you mean?" asked Macbeth nervously, for he was afraid the women were witches.

"Well, it sounds like good news," Banquo joked.

"Hail, Banquo," replied the oldest witch. "Not a king, but a father of kings to come."

"That's mysterious," laughed Banquo, "but it's good enough for me! Come on, Macbeth, Duncan's expecting us."

"Wait," said Macbeth, frozen to the spot. "Where did you get this news? I am Thane of Glamis; but not Cawdor. And how could I be king?" But just then, a passing drift of fog obscured the witches. When it cleared, they were gone.

"Macbeth, my liege!" came a cheery voice. Lord Ross was marching up to them out of the mist. "Or should I say, Thane of Cawdor!" He grinned at them.

"What?" gasped Macbeth. Banquo's mouth dropped open.

"Your new title!" Ross said. "The king's heard all about your fearless fighting. This is your reward. Cawdor Castle is yours! Now, the king wants to see you. Let's go!"

"What can this mean?" Macbeth whispered to Banquo as they tramped along. "What they said came true – Banquo, this could mean you'll be a father of kings!"

"And you could be king yourself," agreed Banquo, "but Macbeth – be careful. Don't be deceived by the words of witches. Duncan is the king, remember."

But Macbeth couldn't banish the thought from his mind. He was Duncan's cousin, and third in line to the throne. Would he really become king? As soon as he got a chance, Macbeth wrote a letter to his wife. He was sure she would know what to do.

My dearest wife,

You will have heard by now of our great victory. Duncan is so delighted with my success, he has named me Thane of Cawdor! So you, my dear, are now the lady of two great castles! But perhaps there is even more to come. You must keep this a secret. When we were returning from the battle, Banquo and I met three strange women on the moor – witches, there was no doubt. They hailed me Thane of Glamis, Thane of Cawdor, and then king! Just moments later, Lord Ross arrived to tell me I had been made Thane of Cawdor. Imagine, my darling – if the rest of their prophecy comes true, you will one day be the queen of Scotland!

I am to meet the king at his palace today, and I will be home tomorrow.

Your loving husband,
Macbeth

The next day, the letter arrived at Macbeth's castle.
Lady Macbeth smiled a satisfied, catlike smile as she
finished reading it, rolled it up and held it to her heart.

"So," she purred to herself, "Queen of Scotland!
But the question is, does that cowardly husband of mine
have the courage to make our dreams come true?"

She tossed the letter aside onto an embroidered
cushion, strolled over to the stone windowsill, and looked out
over the shimmering sea.

There was a loud knock at the door, and a maid burst in.
"My lady!" she panted, "we've just heard the king is coming here
tonight, to pay us a royal visit!"

"Why, what excellent news!" said Lady Macbeth.
"Tell the kitchens to prepare a banquet, and make the best
chambers in the tower ready for our guests."
The maid hurried off.

"Excellent news indeed," Lady Macbeth said
to herself, her green eyes flashing. "I'm sure we'll
make the king's last night very comfortable..."

"My darling!"
Macbeth had arrived.

"Welcome home, my dear!" cried his wife, encircling him with her arms. "My gallant Thane of Glamis, my courageous Thane of Cawdor – and, perhaps, my future royal husband!"

"Ah yes... about the king," said Macbeth. "He's coming to stay, with his sons and all his advisors. We have to get the castle ready!"

"The preparations are all taken care of, my dear. Now all that remains is for us to take care of *him*..."

"I don't know what you're talking about," said Macbeth, looking away uncomfortably.

"I think you do," cajoled Lady Macbeth. "I can see it in your face. We won't get a chance like this again – it has to be tonight."

"No..." Macbeth hesitated. "Let's talk about it another time."

His wife smiled at him indulgently. "You just leave all the details to me," she said, and swept out of the room.

～

"What a lovely spot!" sighed Duncan, as the royal party reached the gates of Macbeth's castle. Dusk was falling, and house martins twittered and swooped around the castle's stone towers and ledges.

"Your noble majesty!" exclaimed Lady Macbeth, gliding across the drawbridge in her blood-red velvet gown. "How delighted we are to have you as our guest! I do hope you'll be comfortable here, since we've had so little time to prepare for your visit..."

"My dear lady, I'm sure we'll have a wonderful time," replied the white-haired king. "I just hope you haven't gone to too much trouble. Now, let's go inside and see your husband." And taking her hand, Duncan stepped across the drawbridge, under the castle's battlements, and into its dark shadows.

The castle cooks had prepared a dazzling five-course feast, fit for any emperor, and King Duncan seemed to be enjoying every mouthful. But, as the wine flowed and the guests gossiped, Macbeth excused himself. He had to think. Sinking onto a stone seat in a remote corner of the castle, he held his head in his hands and sighed.

"I can't do it," he groaned. "I can't kill him. If I knew it was guaranteed to work, then maybe... But Duncan is a good king, and a good man too. He's my cousin, and a guest in my castle – I should be protecting him from danger, not carrying the knife myself."

"What are you doing here!?" whispered a cross voice. His wife was standing beside him. "Don't you know the feast is nearly over? The king's asking where you are!"

"Listen..." said Macbeth, looking her in the eye at last. "This can't go any further. Duncan has blessed us with this visit. We can't kill him now."

"Can't?" Lady Macbeth hissed. "Only a coward says 'can't'!"

"I'm not a coward," said Macbeth. "I risked my life fighting for my king and country. But murder? Murder's not brave, it's evil."

"For goodness' sake!" his wife snapped. "Do you want to be king, or don't you?"

"But what if it goes wrong...?" said Macbeth weakly.

"It *won't* go wrong – not if you don't mess it up! Listen. I'll drug his bodyguards. You'll use their daggers to kill him, then put the daggers back in their hands."

"And everyone will think they've done it..." said Macbeth.

"Especially when we make a huge fuss about how upset we are!" his wife said.

"Alright – alright," said Macbeth. "I'll do it."

"Good," said his wife. "Now get back in that dining room."

~⌇~

That night was the darkest Macbeth had ever known. The moon had sunk below the horizon when he set out across the courtyard, heading for the tower where Duncan slept.

He still couldn't believe what he was about to do. He stopped and rubbed his eyes. When he opened them again, the darkness seemed to swirl in front of him. Something glinted at him out of the gloom. It became clearer, floating in the air near his hand.

It was a dagger.

Macbeth felt himself breaking out in a sweat. It looked so real! He reached out and tried to grasp the handle, but his fingers passed through it. As he drew back his hand in shock, he saw, as clear as day, drops of blood forming on the dagger's gleaming blade.

"No..." Macbeth choked, barely able to speak. "You're not real – I'm imagining things. Go away!" he screamed at the dagger, but it still floated there, taunting him.

Then, through the dark air, he heard a small bell ringing – Lady Macbeth's signal that the coast was clear. Macbeth swallowed hard, and walked in the direction of the tower.

~⌇~

"Come on Macbeth, where are you?" Lady Macbeth mumbled to herself, as she paced up and down the castle corridor. She couldn't imagine what could be taking him so long.

She had already given Duncan's bodyguards a drugged bedtime drink, and left their daggers ready at the foot of the king's bed. Macbeth's task was an easy one.

Just then, her husband's voice echoed from the end of the passageway. "I've – I've done it," he said faintly. "But look at my hands!" His eyes were wide with horror.

"What about them?" said his wife impatiently. She looked down at his bloodsoaked fingers. "Macbeth!" she gasped. "Why did you bring the daggers with you? You should have put them in the guards' hands! Go back at once, and make it look as if they did it!"

"I can't go back – I'm too afraid to look at what I've done – "

"Oh, give them to me!" fumed Lady Macbeth. She grabbed the daggers, which were slippery with blood, and stormed off back to the tower.

"The king is dead!" Lord Macduff's voice echoed around the castle. "Treason! Murder most foul!" His cries brought the other guests, Lord Ross and Lord Lennox, Banquo and his son Fleance, and the princes, Malcolm and Donalbain, stumbling from their beds.

"What's going on?" called Macbeth, emerging from his chamber. His hands were washed clean and he had put on his nightshirt – although he had not slept a wink.

"See for yourself!" Macduff shouted, pointing a trembling finger at the tower. "I went to wake the king and found him dead! He's been stabbed in his sleep!"

"No!" Macbeth hurried up the stone steps to Duncan's room, as his wife wandered out into the hall. "What's all this noise?" she asked innocently.

"My lady, terrible news," said Macduff. "Our royal king is murdered."

"What, in our house?" said Lady Macbeth, blinking in fake confusion.

"It's true!" wailed Macbeth from the top of the tower steps. "King Duncan has been stabbed!"

"B-but... who did it?" stammered Prince Donalbain tearfully.

"His bodyguards, by the look of it," said Macduff.

"And they have paid for their crimes," Macbeth announced suddenly. "When I saw them lying there, stained with guilt, I killed them." Everyone stared at him. "My anger and grief overcame me!" he cried. "When I saw my king lying dead – I had to avenge him..."

"Oh! help me!" squealed his wife, toppling over in a faint to distract attention from Macbeth.

"Look to the lady!" said Banquo, and several lords rushed to her side. "And send news to the palace. We must arrange the funeral and discuss what to do."

As Lady Macbeth was carried back to her bed, and servants were called to attend to the bodies, Prince Malcolm took his younger brother aside and spoke to him quietly.

"Donalbain, we've got to get out of here."

"Why? The murderers are dead."

"Murdoch and McAllister?" said Malcolm. "You don't really think it was them, do you? I don't. They were like brothers to him. They would never have done such a thing."

"You mean it was someone else? Who?"

"I'm not sure. But, whoever it is, I don't think they've finished. We must leave. You stay with our cousins in Ireland, and I'll go to London, until the truth has come out."

"Then people will think we did it," protested Donalbain.

"We have no choice. If we don't get out of the way, we'll be next." And so the brothers slipped away to the stables, saddled their horses, and galloped off into the dawn.

~~

"It's a shady business, and no mistake," mused Lord Ross, as he and Macduff sat outside the castle. "What's the latest news?"

"Well, the finger of guilt points to the princes," said Macduff. "They've run away. People are saying they must have killed Duncan, planning to take over the throne, then lost their nerve and escaped. Though I must say, I never dreamed they would harm their beloved father."

"A terrible shame," said Ross. "So I suppose Macbeth is next in line?"

"It's all settled," said Macduff. "He's being crowned tomorrow."

"Well, I'd better attend the ceremony," said Ross. "Will you be coming?"

"No," frowned Macduff. "It's home to Fife for me. And, to be honest, I think there might be more to this than meets the eye. I just hope Macbeth will be as good a king as Duncan was."

A few days later, Banquo found himself waiting in a large hall in the royal palace. King Macbeth had asked to see him.

"Well, you've got it all, now, Macbeth," he said to himself, as he wandered around the lavishly furnished room. "Thane of Glamis, Thane of Cawdor, and now the crown." He heard footsteps approaching. "But I'm afraid you didn't come by it very honestly," he mumbled, before the doors swung open.

"Banquo, my dear friend!" cried Macbeth. He was wearing his crown and fur robes.

"You wanted to see me, your majesty?"

"Yes," said Macbeth. "You see, we're having a special banquet this evening, and I insist that you come."

"Why, of course," said Banquo, with a false smile. "I could never refuse such a kind invitation. I'm going riding with Fleance this afternoon, but I'll be back in time for dinner."

They both smiled politely, and Banquo took his leave.

"He knows," growled Macbeth, as soon as his old friend had left. "He knows!"

A servant appeared at the door. "The men you sent for, sir," he said. "They're here."

As darkness fell, Banquo and his son Fleance rode up to the palace. They tethered their horses and walked towards the gate, through the deep shadows cast by the palace walls.

Banquo thought he heard a sound, a low murmur that suggested someone was nearby. He looked over his shoulder anxiously. The next thing he knew, three men were on top of him, stabbing him in the chest. Fleance cried for help and threw himself at the scuffle, desperate to save his father.

"No Fleance, get away!" gasped Banquo. "Run – live to avenge my death!" So, as his dear father breathed his last breath, Fleance scrambled to his feet and ran for his life into the darkness.

Inside the palace, Macbeth's guests took their places around the dinner table.

"Welcome to the palace!" Macbeth announced cheerfully.

But he couldn't help looking at the empty place halfway down the table. "Please excuse me for a moment," he said.

He hurried over to the doorway, where a shadowy figure was waiting for him.

"Is it done?" he whispered.

"We killed Banquo, sir," said the man, "but I fear his son escaped."

Macbeth's heart sank. "You'd better go," he said. "I'll meet with you tomorrow."

As he turned back towards the table, pasting a smile onto his face, Macbeth saw something that made his blood run cold. There was someone in Banquo's place.

It was Banquo.

His throat was slit, and his hair was matted with blood. Yet he did not seem to be in pain. He sat very still, looking Macbeth in the eye, and smiling.

"What's wrong, your majesty?" asked Lord Lennox.

"Erm... Banquo?" Macbeth faltered.

"It seems he's a little late," said Lennox. "We're saving this empty seat for him."

"B-but..." began Macbeth. Then fear and horror overcame him. "Don't look at me like that!" he screamed at the ghost. "It wasn't me! What do you want? Get away from me!!"

Lady Macbeth stood up. "I think my dear husband is having one of his turns," she announced to the startled guests. "It's quite normal, he'll be better in a second."

"Can't you *see*?" shouted Macbeth. "Look! He's there! He's right in front of us!"

"I think we'd better leave, my lady," said Lord Ross. "The king is not well."

They all got up awkwardly and made their farewells, wishing Macbeth better health.

"What is *wrong* with you?!" hissed Lady Macbeth as soon as everyone had gone.

"Didn't you see Banquo? He was right there! In that seat... but he's gone now," said Macbeth weakly.

"I didn't see anyone there!" snapped his wife. "No one did! You need some sleep."

"I can't sleep!" said Macbeth. "I've got to get rid of anyone who knows. Like Macduff – he must know, that's why he wouldn't accept my invitation to the feast. I'll go and see the witches tomorrow. I'll ask them what to do."

"Macbeth, shut up," his wife said. "You're going crazy. Let's just get some sleep."

At last she persuaded him to retire to bed. But Macbeth was right about one thing: Macduff did suspect something. At that moment, he was not at home in Fife, but in London, where Duncan's son Malcolm was staying with the King of England. They intended to wage war on Macbeth, and return the throne to its rightful heir.

The following day, Macbeth stood on the cold, misty moor, at the spot where he had first seen the witches. "Where are you?" he called. "Witches, I need to speak to you!"

"We are here," said a woman's voice. As the three figures slowly came into view, Macbeth saw that they were sitting around a huge, black cauldron, adding mysterious ingredients to a bubbling mixture inside.

"We can read your mind, Macbeth," said the oldest witch, "and we know what questions you bring. Here are the answers."

As Macbeth stared, a dark form rose out of the cauldron. It soon took the shape of a soldier, wearing a heavy battle helmet. He turned to face Macbeth, and his eyes glowed as he whispered:

*Macbeth! Macbeth! Macbeth! Beware Macduff!*

"I knew it!" Macbeth said. "He – "

"Silence!" said the oldest witch. "Behold!" The soldier had gone, and in his place floated a newborn baby. Eerily, it also began to speak.

*Macbeth! Macbeth! Macbeth! Laugh to scorn*
*The power of man, for none of woman born*
*Shall harm Macbeth!*

Macbeth began to smile. "If no one who has ever been born can harm me, I'm safe," he said. And then another vision appeared: a child carrying a branch. The child sang:

*Macbeth shall never be destroyed until*
*Great Birnam Wood walks to Dunsinane Hill!*

Macbeth almost laughed with relief. "Well, that's not going to happen!" he said. "I'm definitely safe!" But then he heard a crash of thunder, and to his horror, Banquo's face hung in the air in front of him.

"Banquo!" Macbeth roared. "No! Get out of my sight!" And he slashed at the ghost with his sword. But the witches and the visions had suddenly disappeared.

"Your majesty?" Lord Lennox was riding up to him. "I bring news – Macduff has fled to England."

"Thank you, Lennox," said Macbeth calmly. But when Lennox had gone, he snarled, "I was right all along! It's time to show Macduff who he's up against!"

In London, Macduff was talking to Malcolm, Duncan's son. "Scotland needs you, Malcolm," he urged. "You're Duncan's heir, and you must take what's rightfully yours."

"I know," said Malcolm, "and with your help, I'm prepared to try. We have ten thousand men ready, and we'll set off for Scotland at your word."

"My Lord Macduff," a quiet voice interrupted them. It was Lord Ross.

"My dear Ross!" cried Macduff, striding over to his friend. "What news from home?"

"Bad news," Ross said, looking at the ground. "Macduff, I – I bring such terrible tidings... I am afraid to tell you..." He was trembling, and almost in tears.

"What is it?" said Macduff. "Bad news for who?"

"For you," said Ross. "Your wife, your children... Macduff – they've been murdered."

Macduff's face was white. "My wife?" he asked, helplessly. "My babies?"

"Macbeth's men broke into your castle," said Ross. "I'm so sorry."

"Avenge them," Malcolm said, looking Macduff in the eyes.

"I will," Macduff said, his voice almost a whisper. "I will. I'll kill him."

* * *

"It's like this every night," said the lady-in-waiting, showing the doctor into Macbeth's palace. "She walks in her sleep, talks to herself – we don't know what to do. Look, here she comes." As they watched, Lady Macbeth emerged from her bedchamber in her white nightgown.

"Her eyes are open," said the doctor.

"But she doesn't see us," the lady explained. "She just wrings her hands, again and again, and says strange things. Shh – listen."

"Will these hands never be clean?" Lady Macbeth said, in a hollow, haunted voice. "Who would have thought the old man to have had so much blood in him?" she went on. "My hands still smell of blood. All the perfume in the world will never sweeten them. Wash your hands, and put on your nightgown. Banquo's buried. He cannot escape from his grave."

"I don't know what she's talking about," said the doctor, "but it doesn't sound good."

"Indeed," said the lady, "for all her riches, I wouldn't change places with her. She's seen things she shouldn't have, that's for sure."

* * *

They're coming!" shouted the lookout from the top of the hill. "The English are coming!"

Lord Lennox exchanged glances with Lord Ross. "I'm all for joining the English forces, and helping Malcolm retake the throne," he said.

Ross nodded. "The sooner we get rid of Macbeth, the better," he agreed. "I hear he's holed himself up in Dunsinane Castle. Malcolm's armies are heading for Birnam Wood. We'll meet them there."

In the hall of Dunsinane Castle, Macbeth paced the floor, frowning furiously. "No man of woman born can harm me!" he said to himself, over and over again. "Birnam Wood will not come to Dunsinane!"

A messenger hurtled in through the door, white-faced with terror. "News, your majesty!" he panted. "Malcolm's army is coming – they have ten thousand men, sir!"

"Coward!" yelled Macbeth. "Scared, are you? Well, Macbeth isn't scared. Bring me my sword! Prepare for battle! And what do you want?" he barked, turning to the doctor.

"Your wife is unwell, your majesty," said the doctor quietly. "She's... seeing things."

"Well, you're the doctor," Macbeth snapped. "So you cure her! Now, where's my sword?"

At Birnam Wood, just a few miles from Dunsinane, the English armies had gathered. Rank upon rank of men stood armed and at the ready, their helmets and swords glinting in the sun.

"These are my orders," Malcolm told his generals. "Each man is to cut a branch from this forest, and use it to camouflage himself as we make our way to Macbeth's stronghold at Dunsinane. At my command, we will throw down our disguise, and attack!"

"An excellent plan, your highness," said Macduff.

~

"What's wrong with you?" Macbeth shouted at the few soldiers who had not yet deserted him. "You're cowards, all of you!"

The men shifted uncomfortably in their battle gear, trying to look brave. Then a servant came in. "My lord," he said. "Lady Macbeth is dead. She's killed herself."

Macbeth stared at him for a moment, but he had no time to reply before a guard from the lookout tower rushed in, his face white with shock.

"Y-your majesty," he trembled, "I've just seen something amazing..."

"What? Come on, man, what is it?"

"Birnam Wood – " the guard began. "Well, I know it sounds strange, sir, but I think... I think it's moving."

"Liar!!!" screamed Macbeth. "Come on, outside, all of you! We'll take our chances in the battle! I will not surrender!"

Outside on Dunsinane Hill stood Malcolm's men, disguised by the leaves and twigs of the branches they had cut from Birnam Wood. They had left it almost bare.

"Throw down your branches," Malcolm yelled. "Attack!"

And with a huge roar, the soldiers threw aside their camouflage, and surged down across the hillside to the castle.

For all his evil ways, Macbeth was still a great soldier and a deadly swordsman. He took on all comers, slashing right and left with his blade, until dozens of English soldiers lay dead. But the attacking forces breached the castle, overcoming the guards and forcing their way across the drawbridge. Soon, Macbeth alone was left to fight the ten-thousand-strong army. But there was only one man who could kill him.

"Where is he?" growled Macduff, pressing forward through the throng. "I must avenge my wife and children!" He spotted his enemy by the drawbridge, and as he drew closer, he yelled out "Macbeth! Turn to face me!"

Macbeth spun around. "Macduff..." he said, recognizing his old friend.

"I'm here to take my revenge!" Macduff roared, and he lunged forward.

"Save your strength, Macduff," Macbeth panted as their swords clashed and clanged. "You can't hurt me – I live a charmed life." He dodged and parried, wielding his blade defensively. "Yes, Birnam Wood has come to Dunsinane. But the witches told me clearly – no man of woman born can harm Macbeth."

"Well," snarled Macduff, "perhaps they forgot to tell you that Macduff was never born. My mother died before I could be born." He pinned Macbeth up against the castle gateway. "I was cut from her lifeless body," he added, by way of explanation. "Ready to surrender yet?"

"NEVER!" Macbeth roared. So Macduff raised his sword, gripped it with both hands, and swung it with all his might.

～

"Hail, King of Scotland," Macduff cried, tramping into Malcolm's battle tent. "The battle is over. The tyrant is dead." And he threw Macbeth's head onto the ground, where it tumbled across the earth, and rolled to a stop at King Malcolm's feet.

# Romeo and Juliet

The peaceful calm of a summer afternoon in Verona was shattered. Stallholders ran for cover and parents hurried their children away as two rival gangs of young men brawled their way across the market square. Punching, kicking, and slashing with their daggers, they overturned fruit barrows, smashed shop windows and beat each other to the ground. By the time Prince Escalus's soldiers arrived to calm the disturbance, nearly a dozen of the youths lay injured and bleeding in the dust.

The prince's men broke up the fighting, and soon the prince himself came to survey the damage. Then, looking furious, he addressed everyone in the square.

"This fighting between the Montagues and the Capulets is ruining Verona," he said, "and I'm fed up with it! This is the third time in a month I've had to stop a brawl in the square. If I hear of anyone else taking part in this silly feud, they'll pay with their lives!"

A few minutes later, Old Montague, the head of the Montague family, arrived at the square with his wife. Many years earlier, Montague had fallen out with Capulet, another Veronese gentleman, and their families had been feuding ever since. By now, even their servants hated each other, and fights and arguments between the two sides broke out almost every day.

Montague found his nephew, Benvolio Montague, brushing himself off after the brawl.

"Benvolio?" he said. "It's not like you to fight in the street. What happened?"

"I'm sorry, uncle," said Benvolio. "It started off as a fight between some of the servants. I tried to stop them, but then Tybalt Capulet came along and drew his sword on me, so I had to fight back. Before I knew it, dozens more lads had joined in."

"That Tybalt is such a troublemaker," muttered Old Montague.

"Romeo wasn't involved, I hope?" Lady Montague asked anxiously. Benvolio was a sensible boy, but her son Romeo was much more hot-headed.

"Oh no, don't worry," said Benvolio. "Romeo's been sitting in the park all afternoon, moping. He's been like that for days."

"I know," Lady Montague sighed. "He won't tell us what's wrong with him."

"Look, here he comes," said Benvolio. "Let me ask him. He'll talk to me." So Montague and his wife left, and Benvolio approached his cousin.

"Still in a bad mood, Romeo?" he asked. "What's the problem? Is it a girl?"

Romeo sighed a deep, troubled sigh. "Her name's Rosaline," he admitted. "She's beautiful. I can't get her out of my mind. But she's not interested in me."

"Romeo, you're always falling for some girl," his cousin said. "In a week or two, you'll have forgotten her. Look around you – you'll see a dozen other girls just as pretty."

"Never!" said Romeo, self-pityingly. "Rosaline's the one for me. It's her or no one!"

Just then, an old man came up to them. They recognized him as a Capulet servant, but Romeo and Benvolio knew better than to carry on the feud.

"Can we help?" asked Benvolio politely.

"Oh, sir," sighed the man. "My master's given me this list of people to invite to a ball at his house tonight. But what he doesn't know is, I can't read – and I don't dare tell him. Will you read it for me, and tell me what it says?"

"Of course," said Benvolio. He took the list and read out the names. "It says, Mr. Martino and his family, Count Anselm and his family, Valentine and Lucio, and their families... and Lady Helena, and her nieces Rosaline and Livia."

"Thank you kindly, sir," said the man, and he hurried away.

"So, a party at Old Capulet's house!" said Benvolio. "Sounds like a big occasion."

Romeo was gaping at him. "Rosaline!" he said. "Rosaline's name was on the list! She's going to be at the ball!"

Benvolio laughed. "Well, why don't we go?" he said. "We can wear masks – no one will know we're Montagues. Come on Romeo, it might cheer you up. And when you compare your Rosaline to all the other girls there, perhaps you'll see sense and forget about her." And they set off to tell their friend Mercutio, and to find some masks and outfits to wear to the ball.

～〜

Meanwhile, at Capulet's house, Lady Capulet went to see her daughter, Juliet. She found her in her bedroom, talking to her old nursemaid, who was her constant companion.

"Now then, Juliet," Lady Capulet began. "You know why we're having this ball tonight, don't you? Your father thinks it's time you were married, and he's chosen a husband for you – Count Paris. He'll be at the party, and we hope you two can get to know each other."

"A husband?" gasped Juliet.

"Oooh, Count Paris!" exclaimed her nurse. "He's very rich, you know!"

"Well, I'll talk to him," Juliet said, reluctantly, "but I don't know if I'll like him."

A maidservant knocked at the door and came in. "The first guests will be arriving soon, madam," she said. "My lord Capulet says your ladyships must please get ready and come downstairs."

No one suspected a thing when Romeo and his friends arrived at Old Capulet's house wearing their masks, and were shown into the main hall. Thousands of candles burned in beautiful chandeliers, casting a golden glow over the finely dressed guests and the tables piled high with food and drink. A band was playing on a stage, and a few guests were already dancing to the music.

"This is amazing!" laughed Mercutio. "Come on lads, choose your partners!"

Mercutio was the joker among Romeo's friends. He loved dancing, drinking and flirting, and was the life and soul of any party. But tonight, even he couldn't persuade Romeo to join in.

"I'll just sit and watch," Romeo said sulkily. "I'm not in the mood."

"Life is short, Romeo," Mercutio warned. "Don't waste it moping over a girl. Come and have fun!" But all Romeo cared about was looking out for Rosaline, and torturing himself even more. So his friends left him to it, and joined the dancing.

A few minutes later, the music paused, and Old Capulet
made his entrance. He climbed onto the stage, and addressed the
whole room. "Welcome to you all!" he cried, "and thank you for coming!
Help yourself to the food, drink as much as you like, and make sure you enjoy
yourselves! As long as you're not a Montague," he added with a grin. Everyone laughed,
the band started up another tune, and the party got going.

After dancing until he was exhausted, Benvolio went to find Romeo. "Well? Have
you seen Rosaline yet?" he asked.

But Romeo was gazing like an idiot at a girl on the dance floor. She was tall, blonde
and beautiful, with a dazzling smile, and she was dancing politely with Count Paris.

"Who is *that?*" said Romeo. "She's lovely!"

"Not again!" said Mercutio, arriving beside them. "What about Rosaline? I thought she was the only one for you."

"She's nothing compared to that girl," said Romeo. "Before, I didn't know what love really was. Now I know. This is the real thing."

"Whatever you say, Romeo," Mercutio grinned, winking at Benvolio, and they burst out laughing. But what they didn't realize was that Tybalt, Capulet's nephew, was standing nearby. He overheard Mercutio say Romeo's name.

"So," he snarled. "Those Montagues think they can gatecrash our party, do they?" He sent a servant to fetch him a dagger, but while the servant was gone, Old Capulet came over. "Why the angry face, Tybalt?" he asked.

"Uncle, there are Montagues here in disguise," whispered Tybalt. "Romeo Montague is just over there. I'm going to challenge him and throw him out."

"No, you are not!" Capulet told him firmly. "What did the prince say about no more fighting? And anyway, even if they weren't invited, they're here now, and it's wrong to turn away guests. So if you can't behave yourself, Tybalt, I suggest you leave."

Tybalt was so angry that he stormed out of the party and went home. But his bitter fury did not die down. It burned in his heart, waiting for the next time he had a chance to confront Romeo. He planned to teach that mischievous Montague a lesson...

Meanwhile, Juliet went to find her nurse. She wanted to talk to her about Count Paris – she thought he seemed a little old and stuffy, and she did not really want to marry him.

As she walked alone down a side corridor, she heard a voice behind her. "My lady," it said. "Turn and look at me, for I long to see your beautiful face again."

Juliet turned and saw a tall, very good-looking boy, with a party mask in his hand.

"You are an angel," the boy declared, earnestly. "I don't know who you are, but I've been in love with you from the moment I saw you. Please, let me kiss you."

Juliet had never been kissed before, but since her father was thinking about finding her a husband, she decided she must be old enough. And she would far rather kiss this handsome stranger than boring old Count Paris.

Now the boy was coming closer, and Juliet didn't stop him. She let him put his arms around her and kiss her. They stared into each other's eyes, then kissed again.

"Juliet! Juliet! What *are* you doing!?" It was the nurse, bustling along the hallway in an enormous ballgown. "Your parents want to speak to you about Count Paris," she said. "And you can keep away from her, young sir. I hope you're not getting any ideas."

"Why?" asked Romeo. "Who are her parents?"

"The lord and lady of the house, of course, the Capulets!" said the nurse. "This is my little Juliet!" And she grabbed Juliet by the hand, and dragged her away.

"Oh no, oh no!" groaned Romeo. "She is Capulet's daughter! They'll never let me go near her! Why does this always happen to me? Oh Juliet, my only love!"

"And as for you, young lady, you'd better forget about him right now," Juliet's nurse scolded her, as she tried to look over her shoulder at the boy. "Don't you know he's Romeo Montague? That's never going to work, now, is it?" And she hurried Juliet back to the main hall.

෴

As the party ended, Benvolio and Mercutio, worn out from dancing and full of delicious food, went to find Romeo. They searched the hall, the garden and the street outside, but there was no sign of him.

"He must have gone home early," said Benvolio. "Come on, let's go."

But Romeo had not gone home. Desperate to see Juliet again, he had climbed over the wall into the orchard that ran alongside the Capulets' house. He was hiding there in the shadows as a full moon shone overhead.

Suddenly, he saw a beam of light. Someone had opened a door onto a balcony above the orchard. Watching from behind an apple tree, Romeo gasped when he saw Juliet step out onto the balcony. "It's her!" he whispered to himself. "How beautiful she is! Her lovely face is like the sun, compared to that pale moon."

Juliet sighed to herself. "Oh, what am I going to do?" she complained.

"She speaks! Oh Juliet, speak again," Romeo whispered, straining to hear her.

"Oh Romeo, Romeo..." Juliet said softly, turning his name over and over on her tongue. "Oh Romeo, why must you be a Montague? What's in a name? Give up your family, and change your name – or else I will give up mine – if we could only be together."

Romeo stepped out from behind the tree. "Whatever you wish, Juliet," he called. "I'd do anything for you."

"Oh! Who's there? Is it Romeo – Romeo, is that you?"

"I hardly dare tell you my name, my lady," he smiled. "You don't seem to like it."

"Oh Romeo, it is you! How did you get in here? You're in terrible danger – if the guards find a Montague in the orchard, they'll kill you!"

"I climbed over the wall – I had to see you again," he said. "Juliet, I love you, and I must be with you. I'll marry you, if you'll just give me your word."

"Oh, Romeo!" Juliet knew her parents were planning to marry her to Paris soon. She had to act fast. "Yes, yes!" she cried. "Yes, I will marry you, Romeo, but it must be in secret, for my parents would never allow it. Send me a message tomorrow, telling me where to meet you, and we'll get married as soon as we can..."

"Juliet? Juliet!" Her nurse was calling her from inside.

"I have to go," said Juliet, "but I can trust my nurse, and I'll ask her to help us. Find her tomorrow at the market square, and give her the message. Goodbye, Romeo, goodnight, my love! Parting is such sweet sorrow!"

"Farewell," called Romeo, "until tomorrow!" The door to the balcony closed, and Romeo crept away through the darkness, climbed back over the wall, and ran home.

ᇰᇰ

Romeo hardly slept that night. He was up at dawn, and the first thing he did was visit Friar Laurence. He was a kind old monk, and a friend of Romeo's family. He grew potent herbs, which he used to make medicines, and he could also hold marriage ceremonies.

The friar was in his garden, watering his herbs, when Romeo came along.

"Good morning, Romeo," he said. "You're up early. Or else you haven't been to bed. Been awake all night partying, have you? With Rosaline, perhaps?"

"Who? Oh – no, not at all," said Romeo. "That name means nothing to me now."

"I see," said the friar with a smile. "So – how can I help?"

"Well," said Romeo, "I'm *really* in love this time – but with Juliet Capulet. We want to get married, today if we can. Oh Friar Laurence, will you marry us in secret? Please?"

"What?" laughed Friar Laurence. "Romeo, this time last week you came to me moaning about how much you loved Rosaline! How can you forget her, and fall in love with someone else so fast?"

"This is different!" said Romeo. "I knew as soon as I saw Juliet that she was the one. And she loves me too."

"You're a very fickle boy," remarked Friar Laurence. "But," he went on, "if you really do love each other, I think this marriage might be a good idea. Once your parents get over the shock, your love will bind your families together, and that might put an end to this silly feud. So, just this once, I will help. If you both come here at two o'clock today, you shall be married. And then we'll try to find a good time to tell your parents."

Thanking him excitedly, Romeo hugged the old friar, then ran to find Juliet's nurse.

❧

Meanwhile, Benvolio and Mercutio were searching for Romeo. They needed to warn him that Tybalt Capulet was still on the warpath. He had been to Romeo's house to challenge him to a fight, and when he couldn't find him, he'd started prowling the streets on the lookout for him.

"There he is!" called Benvolio, seeing Romeo weaving his way through the market stalls, looking as if he was in a hurry. "Romeo! Over here!"

"So, you gave us the slip last night!" said Mercutio. "What were you up to?"

"Important business," said Romeo, trying to hide a smile.

"To do with love?" asked Benvolio nosily.

"Of course, what else would it be?" laughed Mercutio. But Romeo was looking serious again. "There's the Capulets' nurse – I have to speak to her," he said.

"What, you're not in love with *her*, are you?" teased Mercutio. "I think she's a little old, even for you."

"Shhh – shut up!" said Romeo. "I have a message for her – I'll meet you later." So Benvolio and Mercutio left, just as Juliet's nurse spotted Romeo and came over to him.

"Now then, young Romeo," she said. "I hope what my Juliet says is true, and you really do love her, for I'll not help with this secret marriage plan unless you have honest intentions."

"I love her with all my heart," said Romeo, "and I've already been to see Friar Laurence. Tell Juliet that if she will come to his house at two this afternoon, he will marry us."

"Oh, it *is* true!" cried the nurse gleefully – for she loved secrets, and she loved weddings, and she couldn't think of anything more perfect than a secret wedding. And although she knew Juliet's parents wanted her to marry Paris, the nurse wanted Juliet to be happy, not shackled to a man she didn't like. So, winking at Romeo, she hurried home to tell Juliet the news.

As soon as she heard it, Juliet, trembling with nerves, told her parents she was going to visit Friar Laurence to ask his advice about her forthcoming marriage to Paris. Then she ran as fast as she could to the friar's house, where she found Romeo waiting.

"Come on, come on," said the friar, as the young lovers rushed into each other's arms. "We've no time to waste." And he led them inside, and began the ceremony at once.

An hour later, Romeo walked back to the market square a married man. After many loving farewells and kisses, he had arranged to visit Juliet that night, climb up to her balcony, and spend the night with her. Now he was going to tell his friends his news.

But, to his dismay, when he arrived at the square, he found Mercutio and Benvolio arguing with Tybalt Capulet.

"Aha," said Tybalt, when he saw Romeo. "Here he his – the very man I was looking for." He drew his sword. "I believe you gatecrashed our party, Romeo," he said, "and we Capulets don't like Montague scum at our parties. I'm challenging you to a duel."

"I don't want to duel," said Romeo. "Tybalt, you and I should be friends, as you'll find out soon enough. Besides, you know what the prince said. No more fighting."

"Too scared for a little duel, are you?" Tybalt mocked him. "I see – Romeo Montague is a coward!"

"Romeo, you can't let him speak to you like that!" interrupted Mercutio.

"Oh, so you want to fight for him, do you?" Tybalt snarled, turning his sword on Mercutio, who quickly drew his own sword.

"Stop it!" Benvolio shouted, but Tybalt lashed out at his enemy, and soon they were both fighting furiously. "Mercutio, stop!" yelled Romeo, pulling his friend back. But as he did so, Tybalt darted forward, and thrust his sword into Mercutio's side.

"Oh, oh, I am slain!" wailed Mercutio, sinking to the ground in a heap.

"No," said Benvolio, "it's just a small cut – you'll be fine." He tried to help his friend up. But Mercutio's face was pale, and blood began to seep from his mouth.

"Mercutio!" cried Romeo, as their witty, fun-loving friend's eyes slowly closed, and his body grew limp.

"Romeo – he's dead..." Benvolio whispered.

Romeo's face was white with fury. He grabbed Mercutio's sword.

"Romeo, *no*!" Benvolio screamed, but there was no stopping him. He rushed forward and stabbed Tybalt as hard as he could in the chest. With a gasp, Tybalt fell to his knees, then collapsed onto his face. He lay on the ground, as still as a stone.

"Romeo, look what you've done!" Benvolio cried, choking with tears. "You've killed Tybalt, and the prince said anyone caught fighting would be put to death! Run and hide, before the soldiers come!"

Romeo stood there helplessly for a second, staring at the terrible scene.

"Run!" urged Benvolio, and Romeo turned and ran as fast as he could back to Friar Laurence's house.

When Prince Escalus arrived with his men, he demanded to know what had happened. Benvolio told him how Tybalt had tried to fight with Romeo. When Romeo refused, Tybalt had attacked Mercutio instead. Mercutio had died, and Romeo had killed Tybalt in a fit of revenge.

"Well, I can see that Romeo was provoked," said the prince. "His actions were wrong, but understandable, so he won't be put to death. Instead, I'll banish him from Verona."

The news spread fast, and when the nurse heard what had happened, she rushed to Juliet's room. "Oh my dear girl, he's dead, he's dead, he's dead!" she wailed.

"Who is?" said Juliet. "Not Romeo? Oh not Romeo, please no, not him!"

"Tybalt!" said the nurse. "Your cousin Tybalt is dead, and Romeo killed him, and now he's banished from Verona!" she cried. "Oh my little one, I'm so sorry!" And she held Juliet in her arms and told her everything that had happened.

Juliet wept for the loss of her cousin, but even more for the tragedy that had befallen Romeo. "I'll never see him again!" she cried. "Oh nurse, couldn't he stay with me for just one night, before he leaves? Please, can't you find him for me?"

"I know where he'll be," said the nurse, drying her eyes. "He'll be at Friar Laurence's house. I'll go there now, and see what I can do."

When she arrived, she found the friar trying to comfort Romeo.

"Banished!" Romeo was sobbing. "Banished from Verona, never to see Juliet again!"

"But that's good news, Romeo – you should be grateful," said Friar Laurence. "You could have been put to death! Now listen," he went on. "Go to Mantua, and I will explain everything to the prince, and ask him to pardon you. With a little luck, everything will be alright in the end."

"You can stay with Juliet tonight, before you go," said the nurse.

"But make sure you leave for Mantua before dawn," Friar Laurence added.

～∽

Before dawn the next morning, Romeo and Juliet woke up in Juliet's room. Romeo dressed for his journey, kissed his new wife over and over again, and said farewell to her.

"We'll see each other again soon," he promised. "I'll write to you from Mantua."

After watching him go, Juliet went back into her room and threw herself onto her bed, weeping. She was still crying an hour later, when her mother came in.

"Juliet, my dear?" she said. "I want to talk to you about your wedding." Juliet stared at her. "Your father wants you to marry Count Paris this Thursday! Isn't that good news?"

Juliet was horrified. "No!" she cried. "I won't marry him!" But then her father, who had been waiting outside, came into the room with the nurse. "What do you mean, no?" he roared. "You'll be married on Thursday, and that's that!"

"You're upset about Tybalt," said her mother, "but the wedding will cheer you up."

They left Juliet sobbing in her nurse's arms. "No," she wailed. "No, no, no!"

"Oh, sweetie – perhaps you should marry the count, after all," the nurse said.

"I will not!" Juliet said determinedly through her tears. "I'm going to see the friar."

Old Capulet had already told Friar Laurence he would need his services for his daughter's wedding on Thursday, so when the friar saw Juliet coming, he knew why.

"I'm so sorry, Juliet," he said, kindly. "I've heard all about your father's plans."

"I'll kill myself," Juliet threatened. "I'd rather do that than marry Paris!"

"No – wait," said Friar Laurence. "There's another thing that just might work. I have a herbal potion that will send you to sleep for two days – such a deep sleep that you'll seem to be dead. If you take it tonight, your family will think you've died, and they'll put your body in the Capulet vault. I will send word to Romeo to come and collect you when you wake up, and then you can run away to Mantua together."

"Give me the bottle," said Juliet. "I'll do it. And thank you, Friar Laurence."

She went home, apologized to her parents, and told them she would marry Paris. Then she went to her room, took a deep breath, and swallowed every last drop of the potion.

∾◡

The next morning, the Capulet household was plunged into weeping and despair. Juliet had been found dead in her bed. The wedding was called off, and a funeral arranged. When everyone had wept over her, and kissed her, and blessed her soul, Juliet was carried down to the icy-cold vault beneath the Capulet chapel, until her funeral could be held.

Meanwhile, Friar Laurence sent a messenger to Mantua with a letter for Romeo, explaining the plan. But Romeo's friends, unaware of the truth, had already sent a servant to Mantua to tell him of Juliet's death. When he received the terrible news, Romeo finally gave in to despair.

"Well Juliet, I will be with you soon after all," he said to himself. "I'll buy some poison and come back to Verona, and join you in the Capulet vault – and there I will lie down beside you, and end my life." He left his lodgings and went to find the best apothecary in Mantua, to ask him for the deadliest poison money could buy.

So, when Friar
Laurence's messenger arrived with the
letter, there was no sign of Romeo. He was already
on his way back to Verona. The messenger searched all over
Mantua for him, then went home to tell Friar Laurence he had been
unable to deliver the letter.

"Oh no," Friar Laurence exclaimed. "That letter was very important!
Oh dear, oh dear... I must go to the vault and rescue Juliet myself. I'll
hide her at my house until I can fetch Romeo." And he ran from his
house, heading for the Capulet vault.

At that moment, Romeo had just arrived in the vault. To his
horror, Count Paris was there. He had come to say farewell to
Juliet, and was leaning over her body, stroking her hair. When he
saw Romeo, he looked furious.

"Romeo Montague!" he snarled.
"You're responsible for all this. You killed
Tybalt, and now poor Juliet has died of grief for him."
"You're wrong," said Romeo. "Get out of my way."
"Stay away from her!" shouted Paris, and both men drew their
daggers. Paris was older and stronger, but Romeo was more
determined. Pinning Paris to the wall, he stabbed him in the stomach. As
he slumped to the floor, Romeo ran to the marble plinth where Juliet lay,
threw his arms around her and kissed her. Then he took the bottle of
poison from his pocket, and drank it down. "I love you, Juliet," he
whispered. Seconds later, he lay dead beside her.
"Oh no, oh dear!" Friar Laurence panted to himself, as he
sprinted down the street.
Juliet moved. Her eyes opened. She was awake. Looking around
her, she saw the cold, dark vault, and knew the plan had worked.
Then she sat up, and saw Romeo. "Romeo!" she cried. She shook
him. Then she saw the bottle of poison, and realized what had happened.
"Romeo!" she gasped in horror. "Oh, Romeo my love! I'll never be parted from you!"
And she pulled his bloodstained dagger from its sheath, and stabbed herself in the heart.

༄

Friar Laurence arrived too late. He raised the alarm
at once, but Romeo and Juliet were already dead.
When Prince Escalus heard what had
happened, he decreed that the young lovers must
be given a joint funeral, and buried side by side.
"Let this tragedy be a lesson to both
your families," the prince told the Capulets and
the Montagues. "It is now time to end your
feud, and live in peace and harmony, so that I
shall never again have to hear a tale as tragic
as that of Juliet, and her Romeo."

# The Taming of the Shrew

"Ah, Tranio," Lucentio sighed, staring up at the spires, statues and beautiful buildings all around him. "What a lovely town Padua is! I can't wait to start at the university!"

"But don't forget, sir, you're not just here to study," his servant panted, lugging Lucentio's cases along behind him. "You must enjoy yourself too."

"You're right," said Lucentio. "As soon as I've enrolled, we'll find ourselves some rooms to rent – and I'll make sure they're suitable for parties!"

They continued along the main street, heading for the university. But, before long, their way was blocked by a crowd of people having an argument. A well-dressed, middle-aged merchant, with his two daughters beside him, was shouting angrily at a group of young men.

"For goodness' sake, Hortensio, how many times do I have to tell you?" he ranted. "I will not allow Bianca to get married until *Kate* is married."

"This is ridiculous!" scowled the older of his two daughters. "Well, I hope you're not expecting me to marry one of these idiots. I'd rather die. In fact, if one of them was my husband, I'd have to beat him round the head with a kitchen chair, twice a day."

"There, you see, Baptista?" the young man named Hortensio said to the merchant. "Kate's such a horrible shrew, no one's ever going to marry her! You might as well let Bianca make her choice. Then at least one of your daughters will be married."

"I have made my position quite clear," Baptista growled. "Now, Bianca, go back inside, and get on with your studies."

"Yes, father," the younger daughter said sweetly. "Don't worry, father," she added as she headed for their house nearby. "I like studying. I don't mind waiting a while before I get married."

Another of Bianca's suitors came forward. "Please, Baptista," he pleaded. "You can't lock Bianca away. At this rate she'll never get married. What a waste that would be!"

"She can get married after Kate is married," Baptista repeated, "and that's final. So if anyone wants to help me find a husband for Kate, please feel free!" And he marched back into his house. After casting a look of disdain at the crowd of suitors in the street, Kate followed him.

Hortensio turned to the other suitors. "Look – this isn't getting us anywhere," he said. "Let's all do our best to find a husband for Kate. There must be someone suitable."

"Someone desperate, you mean!" laughed one of the young men.

"But it's the only way Baptista's ever going to set Bianca free. Come on, let's all agree." And they all shook hands, and went their separate ways.

"Well, well," remarked Tranio when they had gone. "What a terrible shrew!"

"Never mind her!" said Lucentio. "Did you see her little sister? She was absolutely beautiful! And sweet, and lovely, and – "

"Lucentio – you did hear what her father said, didn't you?" Tranio interrupted. "Her big sister's got to find a husband first."

But Lucentio wasn't listening. "Tranio, I think I've fallen in love," he said. "I have to see Bianca again. And I have an idea. Her father said she had to study, didn't he? Well then, she must need tutors! I'll disguise myself as a Latin tutor, and offer to teach her!"

"Wait!" said Tranio. "What about your studies? What will your father say?"

"It will only be for a little while, until I get to know her," said Lucentio. "I know – you can pretend to be me, and go to my classes in my place! Go on, Tranio, please!"

"Well," said Tranio, "your father did say I should help you in any way I could..."

"That's decided then!" Lucentio grinned, and they went on their way.

≈

Later the same day, Petruchio, a gentleman from the nearby town of Verona, arrived in Padua with his servant Grumio. The first thing he did was to visit his friend Hortensio.

"Petruchio! Grumio!" Hortensio cried, when he saw his old friends. "What brings you to Padua? How are you?"

"Excellent, thank you, Hortensio," Petruchio said. "I'm here for a visit. I've inherited a house, and I thought I would take a trip, and perhaps find myself a wife."

"A wife?" said Hortensio. "How interesting. Do come in."

"Yes – it's high time I got married. I'd especially like a *rich* wife."

"A rich wife?" said Hortensio, showing them into his house. "Well, it just so happens I know the perfect lady for you. She's rich, beautiful and single. Her name is Kate." But then he stopped and said, "No, forget it. I couldn't really ask you to marry her. It wouldn't be fair."

"Why? What's wrong with her?" asked Grumio.

"She's a shrew," Hortensio explained. "A grumpy, bad-tempered misery-guts. The trouble is," he sighed, "I love her little sister, Bianca – the sweetest, prettiest girl in Padua.

But their father, Baptista, won't let Bianca get married until Kate has found a husband. And Kate's such a shrew, she'll never find one."

"Grumpy?" said Petruchio. "Bad-tempered? Hortensio, those things don't scare me. I'm looking for a rich wife, and she sounds perfect."

"No, you don't understand," Hortensio groaned. "She's really horrible. Whoever marries her will never get a moment's peace. Why, just this morning she was swearing she'd beat her husband around the head with a kitchen chair, twice a day!"

"Don't you worry, Hortensio. I'll sort her out. I'll tame her! I like a challenge."

"I'd like to see you try," said Hortensio. "You'll never do it."

"I bet you I will," said Petruchio. "Now, where is she? I'll go and visit her now."

"Wait," said Hortensio. "I'll come too. You see, I have a plan to disguise myself as a music teacher, and offer to give Bianca lessons, so that I can see her more often."

Little did he know that someone else had had the same idea. Baptista had already given Lucentio a job as Bianca's Latin teacher, using the false name of Mr. Cambio.

At Baptista's house, Kate was busy bullying Bianca. She had tied her sister's hands behind her back, and was poking her in the face.

"Get off!" Bianca whimpered. "Stop it!"

"Not until you tell me which suitor you like the most," Kate said. "Is it Hortensio?"

"No, I don't like any of them!" Bianca said.

"So, you'd prefer someone richer, would you? To keep you in jewels and fancy frocks?" Kate went on, prodding Bianca's silk dress.

"Owwww! Leave me alone!" Bianca whined.

"Kate, stop that at once!" shouted Baptista, striding into the room. "Bianca, it's time for your Latin lesson with Mr. Cambio, in the library." He untied her, and she hurried away. Then Baptista turned to his older daughter. "Kate, what is wrong with you?" he demanded.

"Why do you care anyway?" Kate retorted. "You prefer Bianca to me!"

"It wouldn't be so strange if I did, with the way you behave!" her father bellowed. Just then, the doorbell rang, and he went to answer it.

Petruchio was waiting on the doorstep with a bunch of flowers. Next to him stood Hortensio, in a schoolmaster's gown and hat, with a fake moustache.

"Hello!" Petruchio said when Baptista opened the door. "My name is Petruchio, I'm a gentleman of Verona, and I've come to woo your daughter Kate."

"Kate? Don't you mean Bianca?" asked Baptista.

"No, Kate," Petruchio said. "I've heard she's very beautiful, sweet and kind."

"Really?" said Baptista, amazed. "Well, erm... please, do come in."

"And I've brought my friend Mr. Litio," Petruchio added. "He's a scholar. He'd like to offer his services as a tutor to your lovely daughters."

"I'm afraid we already have a new tutor," said Baptista. "A Latin tutor."

"Ah, well, I'm a music tutor," said Hortensio. "I can teach the lute, and singing."

Baptista didn't want to offend Petruchio by sending his friend away, so he said, "Well, I suppose they could have a few music lessons too. Come on in."

Inside, Baptista sent Kate for a music lesson with the new music tutor, while he talked to Petruchio. Petruchio immediately asked him for Kate's hand in marriage.

"My dear man, you haven't met her yet," said Baptista. "And you don't really know what she's like. She's quite a handful!"

"I don't care about that," said Petruchio. "Tell me what dowry she brings with her."

"Why... twenty thousand crowns, since you ask."

"Excellent," said Petruchio. "And I have a large house in Verona. So we're all set for a happy marriage!"

"But that's just it," said Baptista. "That's the problem. She won't make you happy at all. It breaks my heart to say this about my own daughter, but Kate is mean, bad-tempered and foul-mouthed."

"Well, so am I!" laughed Petruchio. "We'll make a perfect couple!"

Just then, Hortensio, in his tutor's disguise, came in. His forehead was bleeding. "Kate smashed my lute over my head!" he groaned.

"What a lively spirit she has!" Petruchio exclaimed. "I love her more and more!"

"Oh dear," Baptista fretted. "I'm so sorry, Mr. Litio – why don't you go and teach my other daughter, Bianca, instead? You'll find her in the library." Hortensio hurried away.

"Now then," said Baptista to Petruchio. "I will go and fetch Kate, so that you can get to know her."

While he waited, Petruchio hatched a plan. He would treat Kate as if she were the kindest, loveliest girl in the world. He would praise her sweet voice and her gentle nature. If she was cruel to him, he would completely ignore her.

When Baptista had brought Kate in, and left them alone together, he began.

"My dear, darling Kate," he cried, taking her hand. "I've heard so much about what a sweet, pretty girl you are. But now I can see you for myself, why, I think you're even lovelier than I'd imagined!"

"Shut up, you donkey," Kate snapped. "I won't be fooled by such nonsense."

"You're right, I am a donkey," said Petruchio. "Would you like to sit on me?" And he pulled her onto his lap. She struggled and slapped him around the face.

"Aha, she must love me!" Petruchio cried. "She stroked my face!" Kate scowled.

"And she has such a lovely smile!" Petruchio exclaimed.

"Listen, you fool," Kate said angrily. "I don't know who you are, but you're starting to annoy me. Now get out of our house!"

"Why, Kate, thank you! I would be delighted to stay at your house. How kind of you to invite me."

Kate screamed with frustration and was about to hit Petruchio again, when Baptista returned. "How are you two getting along?" he asked nervously.

"Wonderfully!" said Petruchio. "Kate's agreed to marry me this Sunday."

"I don't *think* so," said Kate furiously. "If you're still here on Sunday, I'll kick you out myself."

"She's joking, of course," said Petruchio. "That's just one of those funny little quirks that I love so much about her. She pretends to be angry, but it's all just a big act."

And before Kate could say anything else, he grabbed her and gave her a kiss.

"Well," said Baptista, in a puzzled voice. "I suppose that's settled then – the wedding will be this Sunday. I'll make the arrangements and invite the guests." And off he went.

Meanwhile, Bianca was enjoying her Latin lessons very much indeed. Even disguised as the Latin teacher Mr. Cambio, Lucentio was very handsome, and soon he and Bianca were spending all their time together giggling and flirting. Bianca liked him much more than any of the suitors who had asked to marry her.

Hortensio, however, was not so lucky. Whenever he tried to give Bianca a music lesson, she spent it daydreaming about her Latin tutor. She begged Baptista to let her have extra Latin lessons, and poor Hortensio ended up spending most of his time with Kate instead – and getting battered and bruised for his trouble.

Finally, Hortensio decided he would tell Bianca his feelings in a love letter. He wrote it out carefully on beautiful paper, folded it up and went into the library, where Bianca was having yet another Latin lesson with the disguised Lucentio. Saying he needed to give Bianca some homework, Hortensio leaned over her desk, and dropped the folded letter onto the seat next to her.

But just then, a maid hurried in. "Miss Bianca!" she said. "There you are! You're to come and be fitted for a new dress, for your sister's wedding on Sunday!"

Sighing and gazing longingly at her Latin tutor, Bianca got up and followed the maid. She walked right past Hortensio's letter.

As soon as she had gone, Lucentio grabbed the letter, and read it to himself.

"You seem to have dropped a piece of litter, Mr. Litio," he smiled. "Dear me. Here, let me throw it into the bin for you." And he tore the letter into a dozen little pieces, and threw it away.

59

The day before Kate's wedding, during another Latin lesson in the library, Lucentio and Bianca could no longer hide their feelings. Gazing longingly into each other's eyes, they finally kissed. And when Lucentio revealed who he really was, Bianca was thrilled. Not only had she fallen in love, but her suitor was a wealthy merchant's son from Pisa!

"Let's tell your father at once," said Lucentio, "and I'll ask for your hand in marriage! Now Kate's getting married, he's sure to say yes!"

"No – he'll be angry with you for tricking him, and he might say no," said Bianca.

As they discussed what to do, Hortensio happened to walk past the library again. Peering in, he saw Bianca and Lucentio hand in hand, whispering to each other.

"Blast!" he fumed to himself. "She's fallen for that layabout Mr. Cambio!" He kicked the wall in frustration. "Ow!" he shouted, and hopped away. There was only one thing left to do. Hortensio could see that he would never win Bianca's heart. There was a wealthy widow who had been chasing him for months. He would ask her to marry him instead.

The next day was Sunday, Kate's wedding day. The maids had dressed her in a white silk wedding gown, and she was clutching a bunch of beautiful blossoms as she, her father, her sister and all the guests waited at the church. But there was no sign of Petruchio.

"Where is he?!" Baptista hissed to a servant. "Go and look for him!"

"I told you he was a fool!" Kate moaned. "And now he's making a fool out of me too! He never meant to marry me at all!" And she burst into tears, completely forgetting that she herself had said she didn't want to get married.

"There, there," her father soothed. "Even a saint would be upset by this."

"He's coming!" the servant shouted, rushing back into the church. "And you'll never believe what he looks like! He's wearing a tatty old jacket, patched trousers, odd socks, a rusty sword and a hat with a hole in it! His horse is lame and infected with worms, and he hasn't even washed his hair! And as for his servant, he looks even worse!"

Just then, Petruchio and Grumio came in. It was true. They were dressed in old, mismatched rags from head to toe, and both looked as if they hadn't had a bath for weeks.

"What do you mean by this?" Baptista demanded. "Petruchio, this is your wedding day! You should be wearing your finest clothes."

"It's me she's marrying, not my clothes," Petruchio declared. "Hello darling!" he said to Kate. "Come on, let's get this over with!" And he dragged her, still sobbing, up to the altar. The priest looked horrified, but Baptista nodded to him to go ahead. He didn't want the wedding to be called off – it was his only chance to get Kate off his hands.

Kate was so confused
and disorientated, she said yes
quietly when the priest asked if she would marry Petruchio.
But when he asked if Petruchio would take Kate to be his wife, Petruchio yelled "Of course
I will, you stupid dolt!" The priest was so shocked he started coughing. Petruchio slapped
him on the back so hard he fell over. Once the ceremony was finished, Petruchio called for
a glass of wine. But, after taking one mouthful, he threw the rest in the priest's face.

"Petruchio, stop it!" Kate whispered. "We should behave properly at our own
wedding!" But Petruchio just smiled to himself. His plan was working. Kate was already
being much less shrewish than she used to be.

"Well, congratulations to you both," Baptista said, pretending nothing strange had
happened. "Now you're married, let's all go back to the house for the wedding feast."

"No – there'll be no wedding feast for us!" Petruchio announced. "I'm taking my
lovely new wife home to Verona! I just can't wait to show her around her new house!"

"No feast?" whimpered Kate, her eyes filling with tears again. "But I'm hungry."

"It's all ready and waiting," said Baptista. "The best banquet money could buy."

"Sorry," said Petruchio, "but we can't make it. You go and enjoy yourselves." And
he swept Kate, protesting and wailing, into his arms, and off they went.

෴

Petruchio's servant Grumio was the first to arrive back at Petruchio's house. He had been
sent ahead to warn the other servants that their master and his new wife were on their way.

"Is she really a shrew, like they say?" asked Curtis, the butler.

"Well, she was, but he's taming her," replied Grumio, and he told them all about
the wedding. "And then," he said, "he hired a rickety old farmer's cart to bring them home.
She complained, of course, saying it wasn't good enough for her wedding day, so he made
her get out and walk! When they get here, she'll be exhausted! But he's sent instructions
for you all." And he told them Petruchio's plan.

When Petruchio and Kate finally arrived, he showed her in and asked her to sit down. Then he started shouting at his servants.

"Where's Curtis?" he roared. "We need some supper! And water, for my wife to wash her hands." A servant brought in a bowl of water, wobbling it so that it splashed on the floor.

"Spill the water, would you?" Petruchio roared. Before Kate could reach to wash her hands, he slapped the servant around the head so that he dropped the bowl.

Next, Curtis brought in a tray of roasted lamb. The smell of it made Kate hungrier than ever. She was just reaching out to take some when Petruchio started shouting again.

"What's this?" he yelled. "This meat is burned! What do you mean by burning my wife's dinner? Take it away!" And he threw the dishes at Curtis.

"Petruchio, please," said Kate, "don't be so cruel to your servants – they're doing their best. The food wasn't all that badly burned. I wouldn't have minded, anyway."

"No no, my dear, I can't have you eating anything but the best. We'll just have to go without food until tomorrow. It's time for bed."

Kate thought that at least she would now be able to sleep. But she was wrong. In the bedroom, Petruchio started telling her how happy he was to be married, and how lovely she was. Hour after hour he rambled on, in a loud voice, clapping his hands and bouncing on the bed as he listed all Kate's wonderful qualities, so that she couldn't sleep a wink.

∾

Back in Padua, Lucentio and Bianca had come up with a plan to persuade Baptista to let them marry. Lucentio instructed his servant Tranio to pretend to be him, and to ask Baptista for Bianca's hand in marriage. Tranio paid an old man to dress up as Lucentio's rich father, Vincentio, and they set off for Baptista's house. When Baptista realized that Vincentio was a Pisan merchant, and saw his fine robes, and heard all about how Lucentio loved Bianca and wanted to marry her, he said yes at once.

But there was no sign of Bianca. She and Lucentio had been listening outside the room, and as soon as they heard Baptista say yes, they ran to the church, and were married there and then.

∾

In Verona, Kate had given up on trying to make Petruchio see sense. Instead she went to talk to the servants.

"Please give me something to eat," she begged them.

"Oh, no – I cannot disobey my master," said Grumio.

"Maybe she could have a cow's foot," said Curtis. "There's one in the kitchen."

"Oh yes please!" said Kate. "That would be perfect!"

"No, no, no, a cow's foot isn't fit for a lady!" Grumio scolded Curtis.

"But I'm *hungry*!" Kate shouted. Just at that moment, Petruchio came in.

"Still ranting and raving?" he remarked. "I thought you'd calmed down, Kate, but it seems you're still a shrew after all. What a shame! The tailor's about to arrive with some beautiful new clothes for you – but they're made to fit a gentlewoman, not a shrew."

"I'm sorry – I'll stop shouting," said Kate quickly.

"Well, here he is," said Petruchio, as the tailor was shown in. "But I can see from here those clothes aren't good enough for my Kate."

"Yes they are – I love them!" Kate cried. "Please let me keep them."

"No, this won't do at all," Petruchio shook his head as he felt the fine silk and velvet dresses the tailor held out to him. "Not good enough! Take them away."

"No – please!" Kate pleaded. "Please stop this. I won't be a shrew, I promise."

"Goodness, is that the time?" Petruchio gasped. "We must set off for Padua! Your father's expecting us for dinner tonight! Go and get ready, dear." Kate did as she was told, as it was the only way she was going to get anything to eat.

In the carriage on the way to Padua, Petruchio decided to torment his wife just a little more. "Why, how brightly the moon is shining!" he said.

"That's not the moon," said Kate grumpily. "It's the sun."

"Dear me, and you said you would stop being a shrew," said Petruchio. "We can't let your father see us arguing. Whatever will he think? Turn the carriage around!"

"Please don't!" said Kate. "I'm sorry. If you say it's the moon, then it's the moon."

"What nonsense!" Petruchio cried. "Look Grumio," he said, pointing to the sky, "Kate says that's the moon! But it's quite obviously the sun!"

"Alright, it's the sun!" said Kate, clenching her teeth. "Whatever you say."

Finally, they arrived at Padua. As they climbed out of the carriage outside Baptista's house, they bumped into a stranger in an expensive-looking cloak. It was the real Vincentio.

"Excuse me," he said in a Pisan accent. "My name is Vincentio. I'm looking for my son, Lucentio. I believe he's married a girl named Bianca, daughter of Baptista."

"Aha!" said Petruchio. "You've come to the right place! Baptista's my father-in-law. Why don't you come and meet him!" And he led Vincentio inside.

When Baptista heard how Lucentio had tricked him, and married Bianca in secret, he laughed. He welcomed his new son-in-law with open arms, and invited everyone to dinner, including Lucentio, Vincentio, Tranio, Grumio, and Hortensio and his new wife.

As they all entered the dining hall, Petruchio and Kate stayed outside.

"So, you're not going to be a shrew this evening?" he asked her.

"Oh no," she said. "I've learned my lesson now."

"Have you?" he said. "And what lesson is that?"

"To pretend I agree with you, and let you think you're in charge," she smiled.

Petruchio laughed. "Well, that will do for me," he said. "Kiss me, Kate."

∾∾

As the party drew to a close, Petruchio, Hortensio and Lucentio discussed their new wives.

"You've definitely come off worst," Lucentio told Petruchio. "You've got the shrew!"

"Ah, that's where you're wrong!" said Petruchio. "I've tamed her! In fact, I'll bet you both a hundred marks that I have the most obedient wife of all!" They agreed, and Hortensio said he would go first. He sent a servant to fetch his wife, but the servant came back alone.

"She's busy talking, sir," he said. "She says she'll come in a minute."

Then it was Lucentio's turn. He sent Tranio to fetch Bianca, but he came back, saying: "Bianca's having some more pudding. She says why don't you go to her instead."

"Oh dear," Petruchio teased. "It seems your wives aren't obedient at all. Kate!"

Kate appeared at his side, and he winked at her.

"I'd like you to tell these gentlemen how a good wife should behave," he said.

"Well," said Kate, smiling sweetly, and winking at Petruchio. "A wife should always be calm, quiet, and good-tempered, and do what her husband tells her. She owes it to him, after all, since he is her lord and master, and works hard to keep her safe and happy."

Lucentio and Hortensio stared at her, open-mouthed. But they weren't the only ones. Everyone stopped talking and turned to hear what Kate was saying.

"Women should never argue with their husbands," she went on, trying not to laugh. "It's rude and ungrateful. Instead, women should obey their husbands, as a servant obeys a prince. It's silly to try to convince men that we know better than them. That will never work!" And she smiled at Petruchio again, and went to sit on his lap.

"Well done, Kate! Kiss me again," he said, giving her a big kiss. "And as for you two, it's time to pay up."

"You've earned it," said Hortensio, reaching into his pocket. "You *have* tamed her! It's amazing! How did you do it?"

But Petruchio and Kate weren't listening. They were staring into each other's eyes, and realizing that they loved each other more than anything in the world.

# The Tempest

"Boatswain!" screamed the captain. "Boatswain!! Take in the topsail! Do it now, or we'll run aground on those rocks! Hurry!!"

The boatswain could barely hear above the roar of the waves and the howling wind, but he knew what to do. "Down with the topmast!" he yelled to the sailors. "Take the topsail in! We'll steer her to starboard!" To his left and right, sailors scrambled up the soaked rigging, the salty spray whipping their faces, while the boatswain hauled desperately at the ship's wheel.

The rocks loomed nearer, and beyond them, against the dark, stormy sky, the boatswain thought he could see a shoreline. There must be an island here that no one knew about.

"What's going on?" shouted an aristocratic voice behind him. He turned and saw King Alonso and Prince Ferdinand. Behind them were the rest of the royal party – the king's brother Sebastian, his advisor Gonzalo, and Antonio, the duke of Milan.

"Shouldn't you be doing something?" shouted the king. "We're rather close to those rocks, you know!"

"Get back to your cabins!" the boatswain yelled, throwing his usual courtesy to the wind. "You're getting in the way – stay below deck with the other passengers, and leave this to us, or else this tempest will be the death of us all!"

"It's useless!" called a sailor from the rigging. "We're doomed! Pray for your souls!" A few seconds later, with a sickening lurch, the ship crunched against the rocks, throwing everyone off their feet. Pandemonium broke out – the sailors shouted farewells to each other, the passengers below deck started screaming, Gonzalo prayed loudly, and King Alonso called for his son Ferdinand, who was suddenly nowhere to be seen. As the boat began to list and sink, Sebastian and Antonio took their chances and leapt overboard, hoping to make it ashore.

"It's at times like this I'd give anything for an acre of dry land – however barren or covered with thorns!" wailed Gonzalo, though no one else could hear him. "Oh, angels above! Please don't let me drown! Anything but that!"

On the island, Miranda was watching the storm. She saw the ship nearing the rocks, and with all her heart she willed the sailors to steer it to safety. She gasped in horror as she saw the mast tilting, the hull breaking up and the splintered wood being swallowed by huge waves. Tears came to her eyes when she thought of the people on board, thrown into the furious sea, perhaps breathing their last breath, never to see their loved ones again...

"Father," she called, turning back towards their house, a hut of logs and branches built onto the opening of a cave. "Have you caused this tempest with your magic? If you have, please stop it. The sailors are suffering!"

Prospero, her father, emerged from the doorway. He was a wise-faced old man, with long, white hair and a long beard. He wore a cloak, and carried a heavy wooden staff. It was a magic staff, for Prospero was a powerful wizard.

"If I had your powers," Miranda said, a little angrily, "I would dry up the whole sea to save those poor people! Why don't you help them?"

"Don't worry, my dear," said Prospero, calmly. "There's no harm done. I did start the storm, but only to help you."

"What are you talking about?" Miranda frowned.

"Come inside," answered her father, "and wipe your eyes – I swear, not a soul is harmed. You don't understand because you don't know who I truly am, or how we came here."

"Then tell me," Miranda said. "You've always promised you would."

"Yes," said Prospero. "You're a young lady now, and it's time you knew the whole story. Can you remember anything from before we came here?"

"I don't know," his daughter replied. "Perhaps I'm just imagining it, but... did I once have maidservants looking after me?"

"You did!" said Prospero. "And more besides – a palace, and a carriage, and little friends to play with. But that was twelve years ago, when you were only three. I was – and still rightfully am – the duke of Milan, a great city in Italy. You, my only daughter, are a princess. Your mother died when you were born."

Miranda stared at him. "So – what happened to us? How did we end up here?"

"By the evil hand of my brother, Antonio," Prospero sighed. "To be honest, I was not a very good duke. I was too interested in my magic books. They took up all my time, so I asked Antonio to help me run the city. But, behind my back, he stole all my power. He was a great friend of the king's brother, Sebastian, and together they persuaded the king that I was corrupt, and that Antonio should be duke instead. It was all arranged, and, one dark night, soldiers came and dragged me from my bed. I took you in my arms, and we were smuggled out of the city. Antonio told the people of Milan we had gone missing, and we were put out to sea in a tiny, leaky boat."

"Then... how did we survive?"

"We owe our lives to an honest advisor in the king's court, named Gonzalo. He couldn't prevent the plan, but he secretly stocked the boat with provisions: food and water, blankets, clothes and candles – and, out of kindness, books of magic, for he knew how much I would miss them. And so it was that we made our journey, and were washed ashore on this island – our home ever since."

"That kind gentleman!" said Miranda. "I wish I could meet him, and thank him!"

"You'll be able to thank him soon," said Prospero, smiling. "That's why I cast a spell to whip up this storm. Using my magic, I saw King Alonso and his followers, including my brother, sailing past our island on their way home from Princess Claribel's wedding in Tunisia. So I simply arranged for them to visit us. This is my chance to put things right."

As he finished speaking, Miranda began to feel drowsy. Her eyelids drooped, and she laid her head on the table in front of her and fell into a deep sleep.

"That's right, my dear," said Prospero. "Sleep soundly."

~⁓

Prospero went outside. "Ariel," he called. "Where are you? Spirit, come near!"

There was a whispering, rushing sound, and suddenly Ariel appeared, darting around Prospero's head. He was an airy spirit – not a fairy, or a ghost, but something in between. He glittered in the sun with the iridescence of a butterfly's wing.

"Ariel," said Prospero. "Have you done as I asked?"

"Indeed, sir," sang the spirit. "I conjured thunder, lightning, wind and rain. The passengers ran wild with terror, sir – fearing their doom, they leapt into the sea!"

"But are they safe, my spirit?"

"Yes, my lord. The king, his son, his servants – all are safe, on different shores around this magic isle. As for the ship, I put it back together, and moored it tightly in a sheltered bay. The crewmen are asleep below the deck."

"You have done well," smiled Prospero. "I have just a few more tasks for you."

"More? Sir, you promised me my freedom!"

"And you shall have it soon. But don't forget your debt to me. When I came here, I released you from the tree where the evil witch Sycorax had imprisoned you. It's only right that you should serve me. And in a few hours, you will be free. Now, you must do as I ask." Then he whispered his instructions to the spirit, who immediately flew off into the sky.

Prospero went back into the hut, where Miranda was just stirring awake. It was time for the next part of his plan. "Come on, my dear," he said gently. "We'll visit Caliban."

Caliban was sitting outside his cave when Prospero
and Miranda approached. He was a huge, hulking creature,
half-human, half-beast. His hair was matted, his shoulders were
hunched, and his long arms hung close to the ground.

"Caliban!" Prospero called. "There you are. Stop lazing about, and
fetch us some wood for the fire!"

"You have enough wood already," grumbled Caliban, with a snaggle-toothed sneer.

"You are my servant, and you'll do as I say," ordered Prospero. He whispered a
quick magic spell, and Caliban felt himself being pinched by an invisible hand.

"Ow!" roared Caliban. "You are a cruel master! You used to be kind to me. I would
never have showed you all this island's secrets, if I'd known how cruel you would become."

"I only treat you like a criminal because you behave like one," Prospero declared.

"Now, fetch us some fuel!" And Caliban hauled himself
to his feet, muttering insults.

Just then, King Alonso's son, Prince Ferdinand, who had
swum ashore from the shipwreck, came wandering through the forest.

"Where is that sound coming from?" Ferdinand asked himself.
"There it is again!"

The sound he could hear was Ariel singing. The spirit's strange,
ethereal voice floated on the air as he whispered:

Full fathom five thy father lies;
Of his bones are coral made;
Those are pearls that were his eyes:
Nothing of him that doth fade,
But doth suffer a sea-change

Into something rich and strange...

"This song is about my
poor, drowned father!" Ferdinand
gasped. "Something magical must be
happening. Who is that? Who is singing?"

"Who's that young man?"
Miranda whispered, as she and her
father watched from Caliban's cave. "I
never saw anyone so handsome!"

He's just a passenger from the
ship," Prospero said casually. Then Ferdinand
saw them, and fell to his knees. "Fair maiden!" he
cried. "Were you singing that song I could hear?
Are you some kind of goddess, or enchantress?"

"I'm just a... a normal girl," said
Miranda, blushing and giggling.

"But – you're so beautiful!" said Ferdinand. "If we could escape from here, I swear I'd marry you, and make you the queen of Naples!"

"Would you, indeed?" interrupted Prospero. "I wonder what the king of Naples would have to say about that."

"I am the king," said Ferdinand sadly, "or I will be soon, for I fear my dear father was drowned in the shipwreck that brought me here."

"So handsome – and a king too!" Miranda gasped, taking Ferdinand's hand.

"That's enough of that," said Prospero, although he was secretly delighted. "This boy could be plotting to take over my island, for all we know. I'd better keep him prisoner, just in case. Come on, lad!" And despite Miranda's pleas, he marched Ferdinand away.

King Alonso, of course, had not really drowned at all. He was sitting on a beach in another part of the island, soaked to the skin, surrounded by Gonzalo, Sebastian and Antonio.

"He's dead, I can feel it in my bones." Alonso groaned. "Oh Ferdinand, what strange fish are feeding on you now? Oh, my beloved son!"

Gonzalo tried to comfort him. "Sir, I'm sure there's something magical about this island. No harm can come to us here. Just look at that lush green grass, and smell the lovely sweet air!"

"Oh yes, what a delightful spot, Gonzalo," said Antonio sarcastically, and Sebastian giggled. "If only we could be shipwrecked every day!"

"It's your own fault, anyway," Sebastian scolded Alonso. He could only be so rude to the king because he was his brother. "If you hadn't decided to marry your daughter to the king of Tunis, we wouldn't be here at all."

"And now I've lost my son as well as my daughter!" Alonso wailed.

"What's that sound?" said Gonzalo. A tiny tinkling, like a miniature music box, seemed to waft past on the breeze. None of them noticed Ariel floating above their heads, playing his magic harp. The music contained a sleeping spell, prepared by Prospero. Sure enough, King Alonso and Gonzalo suddenly felt very tired. They lay down on the sand, and within seconds they were snoozing.

"What's going on?" asked Sebastian. "Do you feel sleepy, Antonio?"

"Not at all," Antonio replied. But it does seem fortunate that they've both gone to sleep at once. In fact, I'd say it's too good a chance to miss."

Sebastian stared at him. "You mean...?"

"If Ferdinand's dead," said Antonio slyly "– and I'm sure he is – then who's the next heir to the throne? You're the king's brother, so it's you. Between us, we'll control all of Italy."

His hand moved to the hilt of his dagger. "Look at them, snoring away – they're as good as dead already. It'll only take a second. I'll kill the king – you take Gonzalo."

They both drew their daggers, and crept towards the sleeping men. Quick as a flash, Ariel darted past and whispered in Gonzalo's ear. He started awake.

"Wha- what's happening?" he cried, waking Alonso up too. "Why are your daggers drawn?"

"Erm – didn't you hear it?" said Sebastian. "That roaring of wild beasts? It sounded like lions, or bears – we drew our daggers to protect you."

"Bears? Lions?" Alonso gabbled. "W-where?"

"Perhaps it's not very safe here after all," said Gonzalo, getting up. "Let's go and find a better place to shelter. And perhaps we'll find Ferdinand too." And they all set off along the beach.

Ariel watched them go. Then he darted off to tell his master exactly what he had seen.

Meanwhile, King Alonso's jester, Trinculo, was wandering alone through the forest. He had been washed up by himself on a rocky shore, and he had no idea where he was, or if anyone else had survived. He looked up anxiously at the sky, fearing another storm might be on its way. When he looked down again, he was amazed to see a huge, human-shaped creature, lying on the ground under an enormous cloak, and snoring loudly.

"What is this?" wondered Trinculo. "A beast, or a man?" He looked more closely. "He's the size of a giant, and smells like a fish!" he exclaimed. Just then, thunder began to rumble overhead, and Trinculo looked at the sky again. "Well, there's no other shelter around here," he said. Reluctantly, he lifted up the corner of Caliban's cloak, and crept underneath.

Soon after, Stephano, the king's butler, came crashing through the woods, clutching a half-empty bottle.

"Amazing! A four-legged giant!" he gasped, when he saw the cloaked shape on the ground in front of him. One of Caliban's eyes opened.

"Who are you?" groaned Caliban. "Not another spirit, sent by my master to torture me!" He started shaking.

"What you need is a drink!" cried Stephano. He put the bottle to Caliban's lips.

"I know that voice!" called Trinculo from under the cloak. "Stephano, is that you?"

"Trinculo!" shouted Stephano, as his friend climbed out from under the cloak. "How did you get here?"

"I swam ashore, of course!" said Trinculo. "I can swim like a duck. What about you?"

"I floated on a cargo crate," said Stephano. "When I opened it, I found this wine!"

"This drink is delicious," said Caliban to Stephano. "You are kind masters! I will follow you, instead of Prospero. And I'll show you all the secrets of the island – where to find hazelnuts and sweet water, and how to catch limpets, so that you'll never go hungry."

"Well, our ship's sunk and our king's drowned," said Stephano, "so we might as well do as you say. Lead the way, monster!"

Outside the hut, Prospero had set Ferdinand to work carrying firewood. His feet were chained together, and he sweated and groaned as he heaved the heavy logs into a pile. Poor Miranda stood and watched, desperate to help him.

"Please don't work so hard," she pleaded. "Ignore my father and have a rest. He's inside, reading – he won't see you. Let me carry those logs for you – just for a while."

"My lady, I wouldn't hear of such a thing!" panted Ferdinand. "I am delighted to serve you, and to do as your father commands. And anyway – having you here gives me strength." He smiled at her, and Miranda blushed again.

Watching them from the window of the hut, Prospero smiled to himself. His plan was working beautifully. He had to do this to test Ferdinand, and make sure he was worthy of his daughter; but soon the test would be over. He turned back to his books. To complete his plan, he knew he would have to make use of his most powerful magic.

"Prospero stole this island from me, and now he rules me like a slave," Caliban explained, as Stephano and Trinculo slurped the wine they had collected from the broken crate. "I want my revenge! If you can only help me to overthrow him, there'll be a reward for you."

"And what might that be, monster?" asked Stephano jokingly.

"When he's dead, you can marry his daughter Miranda, and be king of this island."

Stephano frowned. "And how exactly will we murder this, erm, powerful wizard?"

Caliban glanced around, then whispered: "He sleeps every afternoon in his hut. You can creep up on him, and bash his brains in with a log. I'll lead the way!" And he dragged Stephano and Trinculo to their feet and hauled them off in the direction of Prospero's hut.

⌇

"It's no use," King Alonso moaned, as the increasingly shabby royal party traipsed along the shore. "My poor son is dead, I know it. There's no sign of him anywhere."

"I can't walk another step," Gonzalo panted. "I wish there were something to eat."

"They're exhausted," Antonio whispered to Sebastian, "and with any luck they'll fall asleep again soon. Have your dagger ready."

But just then, they all stopped dead. A banqueting table had suddenly materialized out of thin air on the beach. It was covered with a tablecloth, and dishes of food were taking shape before their eyes. "Your majesty, look what's happening!" Gonzalo cried.

"It – it must be witchcraft!" cried Alonso.

"I knew it was a magical island," said Gonzalo.

"Well – let's eat!" said Antonio. "You said you were hungry." But just as his hand reached out to pick up a treacle tart, there was an almighty crash of thunder, the banquet vanished, and the sky turned black. Alonso, Antonio and Sebastian trembled and cowered as Ariel, in the form of a towering, red-eyed monster, appeared before them.

"Sinners!" Ariel's voice boomed. "You should hang your heads in shame!"

Antonio drew his dagger, but Ariel laughed. "I am a spirit!" he roared. "Your blade cannot harm me. Nor can it harm my master, Prospero. You evil-doers sent him to his death – but he survived, and landed on this isle. Now he has caught his enemies in his web – and as your punishment, Ferdinand is drowned!"

With another thunderclap, Ariel disappeared, and the sunshine returned.

"What is it, sir? – you're white as a sheet!" said Gonzalo. He hadn't seen a thing.

"D-didn't you see it?" Alonso gasped. "That spirit, that terrible angel? Oh, it spoke of Prospero – Prospero, the old duke, who I thought was dead! The spirit was right! I banished Prospero – and that's why I've lost my son! Oh, the shame!"

Finally, following his master's instructions, Ariel cast a magic spell that froze all four of them to the spot. They stood there like statues, unable to move, awaiting their final meeting with Prospero.

Prospero decided Ferdinand had suffered enough. He came out of the hut. "That's enough wood-carrying!" he called. He snapped his fingers, and the chains at Ferdinand's feet melted away. Miranda ran to him, and the young couple kissed each other.

"I'm sorry if I tested you severely," said Prospero, "but the reward is a great one. Ferdinand, you may marry my daughter – as long as she gives her consent."

"I do, I do!" Miranda screamed. She hugged her father, then ran and embraced Ferdinand.

"You are now officially engaged – and soon we will be leaving this island forever," said Prospero. "I want you both to wait in the hut, until I call you. I have some serious business to attend to."

As Ferdinand and Miranda went into the hut, Prospero called Ariel to his side.

"That drunken rabble will be here soon, with their ridiculous plan to murder me," he said. "I don't want them disturbing me. We'll distract them, and chase them away."

Ariel flew up into the sky, and saw Caliban, Stephano and Trinculo weaving their way through the forest towards the hut. He darted back down and plucked from the air a magic rope, which he strung between two trees. Then he conjured up fine suits of clothes, embroidered robes, shiny new shoes and a golden crown, and hung them all from the rope.

Stephano and Trinculo stopped dead in their tracks and stared.

"Come on," growled Caliban, "There's not much time! We must kill him!"

"Wait a moment, monster," Stephano said, gazing up at the clothes. "Look at these! Just hanging here in the forest, for anyone to take away! When I'm king of this island, I'll need fine clothes like these!" And he started pulling them down, and loading them into Trinculo's arms.

"No," shouted Caliban. "We must hurry!" But his voice was soon muffled as Stephano heaped a mound of clothes up in front of his face.

As soon as all three were carrying as much as they could, Ariel called on Prospero. With a wave of his staff, and a spell muttered under his breath, Prospero called up a pack of hunting dogs, with vicious teeth and slavering jaws. Urged on by Ariel, they leapt upon the confused, half-blinded plotters, tore their precious clothes to shreds, and chased them to the other end of the island.

❧

Now all that remained was for Prospero to confront the men who, all those years ago, had tried to rid the world of him forever.

"Ariel," he called, "where are my enemies?"

"Sir, on the beach, and frozen to the spot – but King Alonso still weeps heavy tears. If you could see them, sir, your heart would melt – and you'd forgive them."

"Yes, I will forgive them," Prospero declared. "Bring them here."

While Ariel was gone, Prospero turned and looked out to sea. He knew this was his last day as lord of this island. Soon, he would set Ariel and Caliban free, and return to Milan – and, this time, he would not shirk his responsibilities. It was time to leave magic behind. When this was all over, he would throw his wizard's staff into the sea. It would sink onto the seabed, and remain there, out of harm's way, until the end of time.

"Here they are, sir!" Prospero turned and saw Ariel leading King Alonso, Sebastian, and his own brother, Antonio – all older and more wrinkled than he remembered them – along the shore. Behind them wandered dear old Gonzalo, to whom Prospero and Miranda owed their lives.

"Wake them up," he ordered, and Ariel whispered in each man's ear. They blinked, rubbed their eyes and shook their heads.

"Your majesty," said Prospero. "A pleasure to see you again."

King Alonso stared. "Prospero..." he said in a whisper. "It's true – you're alive..."

"Very much alive," said Prospero. "Thanks to Gonzalo here. My lord Gonzalo, allow me to thank you for your good deeds, fifteen years ago." Speechless, Gonzalo took his hand, and tears fell from his eyes.

"Prospero," Alonso began. "I – I know I did you wrong by giving in to these two scheming traitors." He glanced at Antonio and Sebastian, who said nothing. "Can you forgive me? I'll make amends – I'll give you your dukedom back. Anything you ask!"

"And what's made you change your tune?" Prospero asked, imperiously.

King Alonso hung his head and began to cry. "My dear son – Ferdinand," he sobbed, " – he drowned today. I believe Fate is punishing me for what I did to you."

"Well," said Prospero, a little more kindly, "I know how you feel. For today I have lost my daughter, in just the same way as you have lost your son."

"You too? In that terrible tempest?" Alonso asked, reaching out a hand to Prospero.

"I'm afraid so," said Prospero. Then he turned and walked up to the door of his hut, and opened it. "Come outside," he called. "There's someone here to see you."

Ferdinand and Miranda stepped outside into the sunshine.

"Ferdinand...!" Alonso cried, and rushed to embrace his son.

"They're getting married, you see," Prospero explained. "They're not children any more. They'll be starting a new life – and so will I. I'm coming back to Italy!"

"The heavens send blessings on us all!" cried Gonzalo.

But Antonio and Sebastian still said nothing. Prospero took them aside.

"I know exactly what you were plotting," he said. "But I'll say nothing about it if you two promise to mend your ways, and never plot against me or the king again."

Antonio and Sebastian hung their heads. "I promise," said Sebastian.

"Antonio?"

"I promise," Antonio said sulkily.

"Well then," said Prospero. "That's all settled, then. Ariel!"

Ariel fluttered into view.

"Your last task, my spirit, is to bring the king's ship and crew here, and fetch Stephano and Trinculo, so that we can all set sail. Then you will be free."

Finally, he took his heavy magic staff, raised it over his head, and hurled it with all his might into the waves.

"Come on!" said Prospero. "We're going home!"

# A Midsummer Night's Dream

Theseus, the duke of Athens, was out walking in the midsummer sunshine with his beloved, Hippolyta, the queen of the Amazons.

"Just two days until we are married, my love!" he said excitedly.

"Those days will pass by in no time," Hippolyta smiled. "It will soon be our wedding day, and then we shall be together forever."

"I have arranged all kinds of feasting and celebrations for the people of Athens," said Theseus. "The party will go on all week!" He was about to tell her more, when a citizen of Athens, a man named Egeus, came hurrying up to them, followed by his daughter Hermia, and two young men, Demetrius and Lysander.

"Noble duke," said Egeus, bowing to Theseus, "I need your help. I have arranged for Hermia to marry this man, Demetrius. But Lysander here has been wooing her, and they've fallen in love! Now she's saying she won't marry Demetrius. But I am her father, and she must do as I say. That's the law of Athens, isn't it? You're the duke – you tell her."

"Now then, Hermia," said Theseus. "You know your father gave you your life, and you should be obedient to him. You must marry the husband he's chosen for you."

"But I love Lysander," said Hermia.

"However, you must obey your father," Theseus replied. "That's the law."

"And if I refuse?" asked Hermia.

"If you refuse to marry the man your father chooses," says Theseus, "I'm afraid the law says you must become a nun, and not marry anyone. Surely you don't want that – to be shut up in a convent, chanting prayers all day, doomed never to see another man?"

"I'll take it," retorted Hermia, "rather than marry someone I don't love!"

Duke Theseus sighed. "Take some time to think about it," he said. "I'll give you until my wedding day on Saturday. Then you must make your decision."

"Oh come on, Hermia!" interrupted Demetrius. "Just obey your father and marry me."

"Shut up, Demetrius," sneered Lysander. "Her father might prefer you, but she loves *me*. Why don't you just marry her father instead?" he taunted.

"How dare you?!" cried Egeus. "I'd never let Hermia marry such a rude young man."

"At least I'm not heartless, like him!" Lysander said accusingly. "Until last week, Demetrius was with another girl, Helena, who still loves him. He abandoned her."

"Is that so?" said Theseus. "I think I'd like to discuss this further with you two gentlemen. Let's go and talk in private." And he and Hippolyta left, taking Egeus and Demetrius with them. For Theseus believed in true love, and he hoped to persuade them to let Hermia marry the man she really wanted.

Hermia was left standing in the street with Lysander. She began to cry.

"Dear Hermia, don't worry," said Lysander. "The course of true love never did run smooth. But I have a plan. We can run away, and get married outside Athens – then we won't be breaking Athenian law. Tomorrow night, I'll wait in the woods beyond the city walls, and you can meet me there."

"Oh yes, it's perfect!" Hermia gasped. "We'll come back married, and there'll be nothing my father can do! I'll be there, I promise!"

Just then, Helena came along the street. She and Hermia had been friends since childhood, but now that Demetrius had left her for Hermia, Helena was very jealous.

"Hello Helena," said Hermia nervously. "You look nice today."

"Oh, stop pretending," Helena snapped. "You know very well you're prettier than me. That's why Demetrius likes you."

"Please don't worry, Helena," said Hermia, "for I'm not going to marry your Demetrius. Don't tell anyone, but Lysander and I are planning to run away."

"Yes," said Lysander, "tomorrow night. We're going to hide in the woods, and get married outside Athens. After that, let's hope Demetrius sees sense and comes back to you."

They said their goodbyes, and Helena went to find Demetrius. Despite being asked not to, she had decided to tell him what Hermia and Lysander were going to do. She hoped this would make him grateful to her, and that he would love her again.

Meanwhile, everyone in Athens was preparing for the wedding of Theseus and Hippolyta. In one particular workman's cottage, not far from Theseus's palace, a carpenter named Quince had gathered his friends together. They had decided to perform a play at the celebrations. According to tradition, after the wedding ceremony, the people put on shows and performances around the palace. If they were lucky, the duke would choose one of the entertainments and watch it himself with his new bride.

"Right," Quince announced. "I've chosen the play – we're going to do *The most lamentable comedy and cruel death of Pyramus and Thisbe*. Here are your scripts."

He handed out the parts. Bottom the weaver was to play Pyramus, Flute the cobbler would play Pyramus's girlfriend Thisbe, and Snug the joiner had the part of the lion.

"But I can't read," said Snug.

"That's why I gave you that role," said Quince. "It's nothing but roaring."

"What will I be?" asked Tom Snout, the tinker.

"I'll think of something," said Quince. "And I'll be the narrator. We'll start rehearsing tomorrow night. Not here, because we don't want anyone to hear us and spoil the surprise. We'll go to the woods outside the city walls, and rehearse there."

The woods outside the city were no normal woods. They were magical, and fairies, sprites and goblins lived there. In fact, on the moonlit night when Hermia and Lysander were meeting there, and workmen were planning to rehearse their play, the king and queen of the fairies were there too.

Unfortunately, they were having an argument.

Oberon, the fairy king, had come to Athens on his own. Titania, his wife, had followed him, along with her fairy servants. When she found her husband in the forest, she demanded to know what he was doing there.

"I know what it is!" she cried jealously. "You're here because Hippolyta is getting married in Athens on Saturday! You like her more than me, don't you?"

"How dare you accuse me!?" Oberon retorted. "I won't forgive you unless you give me that boy of yours."

Titania had stolen away a little human boy whose mother had died, to bring up as her own. "You may not have him!" she said.

"But he'd make the perfect pageboy for me," said Oberon.

"Well, too bad," said Titania. "I'm not speaking to you." And off she went with her fairies.

Oberon was furious with her for being so stubborn. "I'll teach her a lesson," he mumbled. And he called for his own servant, Puck, a mischievous pixie.

"There's a magic plant that grows in these woods," he told Puck, "that can make people fall in love in an instant. It has little red trumpet-shaped flowers. Go and fetch me some."

83

"In an instant, sir," said Puck, and darted off. When he had gone, Oberon rubbed his hands in glee. "I'll squeeze the magic juice out of that plant," he said, "and tell Puck to put a few drops on Titania's eyelids when she's asleep. When she wakes up, she'll fall in love with the first thing she sees – whether it's a tree, a stone or a monkey! She'll make such a fool of herself!"

Suddenly Oberon heard humans coming. He made himself invisible and stood aside, just as Demetrius and Helena came into view.

"Helena, just leave me alone," said Demetrius. "I don't love you."

"Please, Demetrius," said Helena. "There's no point looking for Hermia and Lysander – they'll be married by tomorrow. Can't you be with me instead?"

"Oh, for goodness' sake, will you go away!"
Demetrius shouted. But Helena kept following him, and
they both disappeared into the forest.

"That's not very nice," Oberon remarked to himself.
"The poor girl! I know – I'll use the magic plant on that
young man as well, and make him fall in love with her."

When Puck came back with the plant, Oberon squeezed out
the magic juice and gave it to Puck. "You'll find Titania sleeping on
the riverbank," he said. "I want you to go and put a few drops of this
juice on her eyes. And while you're at it, there's a young human couple from Athens in the
forest tonight. When you find them, put lots of juice on the man's eyes, so that he falls in
love with the woman. You'll know them by their fashionable city clothes."

Puck had no trouble finding Titania. She was snoozing on the riverbank, among the
sweet-scented violets, musk roses and eglantine flowers. Puck dropped a few drops of the
magic juice on each of her eyes, and flew away.

Then he went looking for the humans Oberon had spoken of. Not far away, he
discovered a young couple lying asleep under a bush. They were definitely wearing
Athenian clothes, so Puck poured plenty of juice onto the young man's eyes.

Little did he know that there were two couples from Athens in the forest that
night. The humans he had found were Lysander and Hermia, who were already
happily in love with each other.

A few minutes later, Demetrius came striding through the woods, still followed by Helena.

"I've told you, Helena, I don't love you!" he said. "And I don't want you following me. In fact, I'm going to leave you here." And he suddenly ran off into the trees.

Helena started sobbing. What was she going to do now, all alone in the forest in the middle of the night? She was afraid a bear or a wolf might find her and eat her, but she didn't know her way back.

Then she noticed a pair of feet sticking out from under a bush. It was Lysander, lying asleep on the ground! Helena shook him awake.

"Lysander, wake up!" she said. "I'm lost in the woods by myself. Please help me."

Lysander woke up, rubbed his eyes and stared at her. Then the magic juice started to work. A dreamy look of love came over his face. "Helena..." he gasped. "You're beautiful!"

"What are you talking about?" said Helena, feeling confused. "Lysander, please help me. Demetrius has left me alone in the forest and I don't know my way home."

"I'll kill him for doing that to the woman I love!" said Lysander.

"What do you mean?" asked Helena. "You love Hermia, not me."

"I'm tired of Hermia," Lysander declared. "She's nothing compared to you."

"You're teasing me!" said Helena crossly. "Why are you doing this? You and Hermia came here to get married!"

"Never mind her," said Lysander. "I'm coming with you."

And he stood up and tried to kiss Helena. She ran away, but Lysander followed her through the moonlit forest, constantly declaring his love for her.

After a while, Hermia woke up to find herself lying under the bush alone.

"Lysander...?" she said. "Are you there?" But Lysander was gone.

"Lysander!" she cried. "Oh, where can he be!" She crawled out from under the bush, and hurried away to look for him.

Near where Titania was sleeping, the workmen had arrived to rehearse their play by moonlight. Hidden in a tree, Puck decided to watch them.

"Is everyone here?" asked Quince. "Right, let's get started. We'll use this piece of grass for a stage. Behind that bush can be backstage. Bottom, you come on first, as Pyramus."

Bottom stepped forward. "My first line is 'Oh Thisbe mine, I'll kiss you through the wall,'" he read. "But there's no wall."

"Oh dear," said Quince. "Someone will have to play the wall. Snout, you be the wall." Snout came forward and spread his arms out.

"The wall has a chink in it, which the lovers speak through," said Quince. "You'll have to use your fingers to make the chink."

Snout spread out his fingers so that Bottom could look through.

"Now Flute, you are Thisbe," said Quince. "You speak to Pyramus through the wall."

Flute read his first line. "'The wall's too thick, I can't reach your lips at all!'" he squeaked in a high voice.

"Roooooaarrrrr!" roared Snug, pretending to be the lion. Bottom nearly jumped out of his skin.

"No, no," said Quince. "You don't start roaring yet."

"The lion is too frightening," said Bottom. "The ladies in the audience will think it's a real lion. I think the lion should introduce himself, and explain he's really an actor."

"Alright, alright!" said Quince, getting annoyed. "We'll do the next scene, with Thisbe and the lion. Bottom, you go backstage." Bottom looked puzzled.

"Behind the bush!" shouted Quince.

"Dear me," Puck said to himself, up in the tree. "They really are terrible. They need a little magic to liven things up!" So he cast a spell on Bottom to turn his head into a donkey's head.

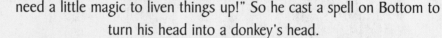

When Bottom emerged from behind the bush, the others were terrified.

"It must be magic..." whispered Quince. "There must be evil spirits in the woods! Run away!" And they all ran for their lives, leaving Bottom by himself in the forest.

"What's wrong?" he called. "What's the matter?" His voice sounded very strange. He wandered off through the trees, calling again and again for his friends. Puck followed him, darting from tree to tree, to see what would happen.

Before long,
Bottom stumbled past the
flowery riverbank where Titania was sleeping.
"Quince! Flute! Snug!" he shouted. "Where are you?"
Titania stirred awake. "What angel wakes me from my flowery bed?" she
sighed. Then she saw Bottom's long muzzle, donkey teeth, and huge donkey ears.
"What a handsome man!" Titania cried. "Oh, stranger, please stay with me,
and never leave my side, for I love you with all my heart!"
"But I must find my way out of these woods and go home," said Bottom.

"No – don't leave," Titania pleaded. "I am the queen of the fairies, and if you stay here with me, you shall have fairy servants to wait on you, and eat wild berries and peaches, and sleep on a bed of flowers!" She called her fairies, and before Bottom knew what was happening, they cast a spell to put him in a trance, and led him away.

Then Oberon came along, looking for his wife. "I wonder if that magic plant juice has worked?" he said.

"It's worked a treat, sir!" called Puck, flying down from his tree. He explained all about how he had given Bottom a donkey's head, and how Titania had seen him and fallen in love with him.

"Excellent!" Oberon grinned, clapping his hands. "It's even better than I imagined! And the Athenian – it worked on him too?"

"Yes sir, I found them sleeping side by side, and put the juice on his eyes," said Puck. "When he wakes he'll certainly see her before anyone else."

"Oh look! Here they come!" said Oberon, as Hermia appeared with Demetrius.

"Well – that's the woman I saw," said Puck, "but it's not the same man."

"Please, just tell me where Lysander is," Hermia begged Demetrius. She had bumped into him while searching for Lysander.

"I don't know where your precious Lysander is," said Demetrius.

"He disappeared while I was asleep," said Hermia, "but I know he wouldn't leave me. What if he was eaten by a bear – or even murdered! Oh Demetrius, it wasn't you, was it? You haven't killed Lysander so that you can marry me? Is that why you came to the forest?"

"Of course not!" said Demetrius angrily.

"Then I must find him," said Hermia, and she ran off into the woods.

"I'm exhausted," said Demetrius to himself. "And this riverbed looks like a good place for a snooze." He lay down and fell asleep.

"Oh no," said Oberon. "Puck, you've made a mistake. This is the man you were meant to find. Now you go and find the other woman, and I will put the juice on this man's eyes, and we'll get them together."

Puck set off, and Oberon squeezed some magic plant juice onto the sleeping Demetrius's eyes.

In a flash, Puck was back, bringing Helena and Lysander with him. "Stop teasing me, Lysander!" Helena was saying. "I know you don't love me."

"But I *do*," he replied, "more than I ever loved Hermia. I can't take my eyes off you."

"Demetrius!" cried Helena, seeing Demetrius asleep on the ground. She ran over and shook him awake. Just as Lysander had done, he stared at her with a dreamy look in his eyes. "Helena..." he gasped. "How beautiful you are. I adore you. Oh Helena – be mine!"

"Stop it!" shouted Helena. "Now you're both teasing me! It's not funny!"

"Wait a minute," said Lysander. "Demetrius, I thought you wanted to marry Hermia. Well you can have her. Helena's mine."

"I thought *you* loved Hermia," said Demetrius. "Look, here she comes."

"Lysander?" called Hermia. "Where have you been? Why did you desert me?"

"Why would I stay with you," said Lysander, "when I love Helena?"

Hermia stared at him in horror. Before she could say anything, Demetrius gave Lysander a shove. "No, *I* love Helena," he insisted.

"You're in on this," Helena accused Hermia. "You set them up to say they love me, just out of spite because you want to mock me."

"I didn't!" Hermia exclaimed. "Lysander, stop this. Stop mocking Helena."

"I'm not mocking," said Lysander. "I truly love her."

"No, *I* love her," said Demetrius. "And I'll fight you for her, Lysander. Let's go and find a good place to have a duel. The winner can have Helena."

"Certainly," Lysander replied, and they set off. Hermia and Helena glowered at each other. Then Helena turned and followed the men, and Hermia went after her.

❧

"This mess is all your fault," Oberon said to Puck.

"No it's not!" Puck protested. "I did what you told me, and found a couple wearing Athenian clothes. I didn't know there were two couples!"

"Well, we'd better sort it out," Oberon sighed. "Go and follow them, and before they can start a duel, whip up a thick fog, so they can't see each other. Send them to sleep, then take this herb, and crush its juice into Lysander's eyes. It will undo the magic. With any luck, he'll love Hermia again, and they can all go back to Athens. Meanwhile," he went on, "I'll go and see how that wife of mine is doing. Perhaps I'll forgive her and undo the spell on her too." He left, taking some of the herb that could undo the love spell. Meanwhile, Puck quickly found the young Athenians and did as he was told. He filled the air with fog, sent all four of them to sleep, and put the juice on Lysander's eyes.

"Titania!" Oberon called. "Oh Titania, my dearest!" He was sure he could hear her voice. He peered around a corner, and saw Titania lying in a flowery glade, tying daisy chains around Bottom's ears.

"Let me decorate your beautiful head with blossoms, my love, and kiss your lovely large ears," she sighed, kissing him again and again.

"Peaseblossom?" called Bottom, and one of the fairies came forward. "Scratch my head, would you?" Bottom said. "And Cobweb? Play me some of that nice fairy music."

"Would you like something to eat, my darling?" Titania suggested.

"It's funny you should ask," Bottom replied, "because I have a strange craving for oats. Or hay! I could fancy some hay."

"I can send the fairies to fetch you some nuts and berries," Titania offered.

"I'd rather have hay," said Bottom. "But actually, now I'm feeling very sleepy. I think I'll have a snooze."

"We'll lie down together, my love," said Titania. Soon they were both asleep.

Just then, Puck arrived. "Look at Titania!" said Oberon. "I feel sorry for her now. I'll undo the spell." He put the herb juice onto her eyes, and she woke up, looking confusedly at Bottom. Then she looked up and saw Oberon.

"Hello, dear," she said. "What a strange night I've had! I thought I was in love with a donkey!"

"You mean that fellow there? Well, he *is* very handsome," Oberon smirked.

"What a fool I've been!" cried Titania. "Please forgive me!"

"Of course I forgive you, my love," said Oberon. "Puck, restore this poor workman to normal, and make sure he and those four young lovers stay in a deep sleep until morning. When they wake up, they'll think everything that's happened was just a midsummer night's dream."

"I will," replied Puck, "but sir, it's nearly dawn. Daytime is no time for fairies."

"You're right," said Oberon. "Come, my dear, it's time for us to leave. Tonight we'll go to Athens together, to give the duke's wedding our magical blessing." He led Titania away by the hand, and they smiled at each other, their fight forgotten.

In the morning, when Egeus found Hermia was
missing, he guessed what had happened and ran to tell Duke Theseus. As the
sun rose, they set off for the forest to look for Hermia and Lysander.

As they walked through the trees, Theseus spotted the young couples asleep
on the ground. "Why, here they are, safe and sound!" he laughed.

"Look, Demetrius is here too," said Egeus, "and Helena! What's going on?"

"Let's wake them up and find out," said Theseus. "After all, I have a question for
your daughter. Today is my wedding day, so it's time for Hermia to make her
decision."

He shook both couples awake. "Good morning," he said. "What are you all
doing here?"

Lysander sat up, looking very puzzled. He rubbed his eyes. "My lord, in truth I
don't know how we got here," he said. "All I remember is, Hermia and I were
going to run away, to get married outside Athens. But instead, we must have
been asleep, for I have had all kinds of strange dreams. But at least my
darling Hermia is safe." He hugged her. Hermia was relieved to find
Lysander really did still love her.

"It's as I thought!" said Egeus.
"They ran away. They would have married
behind my back! And behind yours too, Demetrius."
"Sir, I must explain," said Demetrius.
"Helena told me they had run away. So I followed them,
and she followed me. I don't know what happened, but
now I find my feelings are all for her – for my dear Helena.
She was my first love, and now I love her again." He turned
and kissed her, to her delight.
"Well that's settled then," said Theseus. "Both these couples
shall marry for love. And they shall marry today, and share the
wedding feast with me and Hippolyta. Come on, let's hurry back
to Athens. The wedding is at noon!"
Meanwhile, Bottom the weaver woke up and scratched his
head, which was back to normal. "That was an odd dream," he
said. "Oh!" he cried, remembering the play. He jumped to his feet.
"Quince! Snug! Flute!" he called. "Don't put on the play without
me!" And he set off for Athens, running as fast as he could.

In Quince's house, the workmen were all sitting around, looking miserable.

"We can't put on the play without Bottom," said Flute.

"And I was so looking forward to playing the lion," complained Snug.

Snout came in. "He's not at his house," he said. "There's no sign of him."

"The goblins must have stolen him away," said Quince. "Poor Bottom!"

"I'm here!" Bottom appeared at the door. "Don't start without me!"

"Bottom!" they all cried. "What happened? Where have you been?"

"I'll tell you later," said Bottom. "There's no time now! The duke has already gone to the temple! Soon the wedding will be over, and the entertainment will begin! Quick – let's go!" They all jumped up, pulled on their costumes and crowded out of the door.

～

Duke Theseus emerged from the temple with his bride, Duchess Hippolyta, and the two other happy couples. "Now then," he announced to the crowd. "We'll all go back to my palace to see some shows before the feast. What is there to choose from?"

"Well sir," said his servant, Philostrate. "There's an orchestra of harpists..."

"That sounds a bit boring," said Theseus.

"...or a political satire, about the Spartan War?"

"Not quite right for a wedding," Theseus remarked.

"Or how about a play – a comic tragedy, performed by a bunch of workmen?"

"Now that sounds like fun," smiled Hippolyta.

"I'll let my wife be the judge," said Theseus. "The play it shall be!"

And so, when they came to the palace, Philostrate called the workmen forward to perform their play. Bursting with excitement, their half-tied costumes fluttering in the summer breeze, they jostled up onto the stage set up outside the palace. The wedding party took their seats in front, and the people of Athens crowded around to watch.

Quince played a fanfare on a trumpet, and everyone stopped talking. Then he stepped forward and announced:

> *We plan to play our parts, and get them right,*
> *And put a show on, all for your delight!*

Then the actors came on. Bottom was dressed as Pyramus, and Flute was wearing a dress and a blonde wig to play Thisbe. Snout wore a costume made of two sheets of wood, painted with bricks and covered with clumps of moss. Quince declared:

*Our play's a tale of love, despair and misery,*
*Between these lovers, Pyramus and Thisbe,*
*They love each other, but their love's forbidden,*
*And from their parents they must keep it hidden.*

There was a silence until Quince nudged the wall, and Snout remembered his lines.

*I am Thisbe's father's garden wall,* he said.
*I have a chink, through which the lovers call,*
*Look, here they are! They come here every night*
*To meet in secret by the moon's bright light.*

*Oh Thisbe mine!* cried Bottom. *I'll kiss you through the wall!*

Flute, playing Thisbe, put his lips to the chink between Snout's fingers.

*The wall's too thick, I can't reach your lips at all!* he wailed.

*Then let us meet in the graveyard instead,* said Bottom.
*No one will see us there, for they're all dead!*

Theseus was laughing his head off. "The wall is excellent," he said.
"Yes," said Demetrius, "it's the best talking wall I've seen in a long time."
"Shhh," said Quince. "Now they're going to meet in the graveyard."
Flute came back on in his dress and wig, and squeaked:

*Where is Pyramus? He said he'd be here.*
*He'd better hurry, for the dawn draws near.*

Now Snug appeared in his lion costume. He turned to the audience and announced:

*Ladies, don't worry, for I'm just a man*
*Playing a fierce lion as well as I can!*

Then he chased Flute around the stage until the whole audience was laughing. At last, Snug grabbed Flute's cloak, and Flute ran off the stage. Quince came forward and explained:

*Chased by the lion, she's managed to escape*
*But look! She's left behind her velvet cape!*
*The fierce lion grabs it with his claws*
*And chews and tears it with his bloodstained jaws.*

Snug dropped the cape, and left the stage to wild applause. Then Bottom came on.

*Thisbe? Thisbe? Oh no, I heard a roar!*
*And here's her cape, all bloodstained, ripped and tore!*
*She's dead! Oh woe is me! I must die too!*
*I'll stab myself right now, no more ado.*

Taking out a knife, Bottom pretended to stab himself, squirted fake blood all over the stage, and fell to the ground with a thud. Theseus almost fell off his chair laughing, but Quince shushed him again. "This is the best part!" he whispered "Thisbe's tragic speech!"
Flute reappeared in his bedraggled dress, and screamed at the body on the ground.

*Oh Pyramus! My dear!*
*I hoped to meet him here,*
*But now I find, instead*
*My Pyramus is dead!*
*He was so brave and true,*
*And sweet, and handsome too –*
*He had such nice pink cheeks*
*And his eyes were green, like leeks.*
*Now I shall use his knife*
*To end my unhappy life!*

Stabbing himself under the arm, Flute collapsed in a heap on top of Bottom.
"The end!" cried Quince, and everyone clapped and cheered loudly. The actors all came onstage and took a bow, and Theseus stepped up and congratulated them.
Then, when the clapping and cheering had died down, Theseus led everyone into his palace, for the biggest, most extravagant wedding feast they had ever seen. And because they had all married for love – or was it because the fairy king and queen flew invisibly over their heads, and blessed them with magic charms? – Theseus and Hippolyta, Hermia and Lysander, and Helena and Demetrius all lived happily ever after.

# Hamlet

In a gloomy, tapestry-lined room in Elsinore Castle, Hamlet, Prince of Denmark sat alone, his head in his hands, wishing with all his might that this wasn't happening.

"My poor father has barely been dead a month!" he groaned. "My mother should be deep in mourning – not celebrating a second marriage so soon! And *certainly* not to Uncle Claudius! How could she do this!?"

Hamlet's Uncle Claudius was his father's brother. And now, since Claudius had married the queen, he was the new king as well. Just a few minutes ago, the newlyweds had been in the room with their attendants, and Hamlet had trembled with rage to hear Claudius speaking about his dear departed father.

"Ah yes, what a wonderful king he was," Claudius had declared. "How we miss him! I only hope I can be half as good a king as him. And I hope I can be a good husband, too!" he had smirked, grinning at his new wife.

"Now then, we've business to deal with," he went on pompously. "The Norwegians are still making trouble and I intend to deal with them once and for all. I'm sending the king of Norway a letter to tell him to surrender." He handed the letter to a servant.

"Do cheer up, Hamlet," Queen Gertrude had said, seeing her son's scowling face.

"Yes, boy, it's time you stopped this silly moping over your father," Claudius added. "It has been a month, you know. And as for your plans to go back to your studies in Germany, I don't think it's a good idea. You're better off here, where you can be a comfort to your mother."

And away they went. Left alone in the room, Hamlet couldn't help burning with rage and indignation every time he thought about Claudius.

"Hamlet?" Hamlet's best friend Horatio stuck his head around the door, then he came in. With him were two of the castle guards, Barnardo and Marcellus.

"Horatio!" Hamlet stood up and clasped his friend's hand. "Excuse my bad mood," he said. "I'm just feeling a little confused. Funerals, weddings..."

"They were quite close together, weren't they?" said Horatio sympathetically.

"Close together! They were so close together, we had the leftovers from the funeral dinner at the wedding feast! It's an insult to my father's memory."

"Yes, he was a great man, and a good king," said Horatio. "I'm so sorry, Hamlet."

The prince sighed sadly. "We won't see his like again," he said.

"Well," Horatio said, "That's what I wanted to talk to you about. We – the guards and I – we think we *did* see him."

"What!? Where? Tell me!"

"Last night, on the battlements. Barnardo and Marcellus were keeping watch, and they saw a ghost. They fetched me to come and see and – Hamlet, it was your father."

"We've seen it these past three nights, sir," added Marcellus.

Hamlet was pale and shaking. "Didn't you... speak to it?"

"I tried," said Horatio, "but it didn't answer. I think it wants to speak to you."

∾

As midnight struck, Hamlet stood on the battlements with Horatio and the guards. Below them, lights burned in the castle where King Claudius was staying up late, drinking with his courtiers. But the battlements were swathed in darkness. From beyond the cliffs came the churning sound of the sea and across the courtyard, a distant bell chimed.

"That's the midnight bell," said Marcellus nervously.

"This is when it usually appears," Horatio said.
Suddenly he pointed. "Look!"

At first it seemed like just a faint glow farther along the walkway. But as the three men stared, it glided towards them, taking the form of an old man in full battle gear.

As the ghost came even closer, Hamlet saw that its sword, its helmet, its thick beard and its deep, kind, glinting eyes were those of his father, the dead king.

"Father...?" said Hamlet, but his voice came out as a whisper. "Why... what are you doing here? Why don't you rest peacefully in your grave?"

The ghost slowly reached out a glowing hand, and beckoned him.

"It wants you to go with it," Horatio said quietly.

Marcellus grabbed Hamlet's arm. "Don't go, sir!" he pleaded.

"I will go," Hamlet insisted. "This is my father. He wants to talk to me." And he pulled away from his friends and walked towards the ghost. The night seemed to grow even darker as he stumbled along the walkway, steadying himself on the stone ramparts.

"Father!" he called.
"What do you want?"

The ghost stopped and turned to him. It
stared into his eyes with a sadness Hamlet could
hardly bear. Then it began to speak.

"I am your father's ghost," it said. "I am doomed to
walk the battlements each night, and suffer torment by day, until
the wrongs done against me are put right."

"Wrongs? What do you mean?"

"If you ever loved your father –"

"Of course I did, with all my heart..."

" – then you must avenge his murder."

"Murder?" Hamlet felt his knees go weak.

"A murder most foul, cruel and unnatural," the ghost went on. "They told you it
was an accident, didn't they? They said I was bitten by a snake, as I slept in the orchard."

"Yes..." Hamlet replied.

"It's not true!" hissed the ghost. "I was sleeping in the orchard, but there was no
adder, no creeping viper. The snake that took my life now wears my crown."

"My uncle!"

"He loved the queen, you see, and she loved him. And so that he could be with
her, and take my throne, my brother killed me. He came into the orchard while I was
asleep, and secretly poured a vial of deadly poison into my ear. And so I was murdered,
without even a chance to say farewell. Avenge my death, Hamlet! Goodbye! Remember me!"

~∽

Hamlet knew the only way to avenge his father's murder was to kill Claudius. But
how could he kill his uncle, who was now the king? How could he be sure he would succeed?
Even worse, what if he had imagined the ghost's words, and Claudius was innocent?

He decided to wait for a while. He would try to find out more about what had
happened, and he would only kill Claudius when he was certain it was the right thing to
do. Meanwhile, he would pretend to be insane with grief, in order to disguise his true
plans.

Life at the castle soon became unbearable. Every time Hamlet saw Claudius, he was tortured by images of him heartlessly pouring the poison into his poor father's ear. And every time he saw his mother, his heart filled up with rage, and he longed to tell her that he knew all about what had happened. To hide his furious feelings, he behaved more and more strangely, and everyone started to wonder what was wrong with the prince.

Ophelia was more upset than anyone. For the past year, she had thought Hamlet loved her. He had sent her flowers and love letters, and when he was at home, he had walked with her in the gardens and told her she was beautiful. She'd even started to think he might ask her to marry him. But since his father had died, a change had come over him.

Ophelia sighed, choosing a new thread for the embroidery she was finishing. She should have known. Her father Polonius, the Lord Chamberlain, had told her to be careful. So had her brother Laertes, before he set off for France.

"Don't forget, Hamlet's the Prince of Denmark," Laertes had said. "He'll probably marry some princess from another royal family – not the Lord Chamberlain's daughter."

"That's right," said her father. "Don't pin your hopes on him. In fact, I think you should send those love letters back."

But Hamlet never sent love letters now. These days, they hardly spoke to each other. He used to be so kind and friendly. Now, he had no time for her.

Ophelia looked down sadly at the pattern of intertwined daisies and buttercups she was stitching. Just then, the door of her chamber creaked, and she glanced up again.

It was Hamlet. But he was not dressed for a visit to a lady. His shirt hung loosely to his knees, his legs were bare, and his stockings flapped around his ankles. His hair was messy, and his eyes were staring so wildly, they almost popped out of his head.

"Hamlet... how are you?" she began politely. But instead of replying, Hamlet came and grabbed her wrist, squeezing it so hard that she gasped in pain. He leaned closer, staring into her eyes as if he couldn't tell who she was. Finally, he sighed deeply, and turned to leave – but kept looking at her, over his shoulder, until the door closed between them.

Rubbing her sore wrist and fighting back tears, Ophelia hurriedly put away her sewing, and went to find her father.

"Oh dear," said Polonius, when she told him what had happened. "Perhaps he is in love with you, after all. That must be it! He's gone insane with love for you! I must go and tell the king – he's been wondering what the problem was!"

"But what shall I do?" pleaded Ophelia. It was too late. Her father had gone.

❧

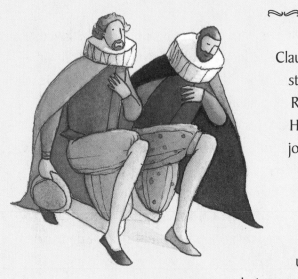

Claudius was very concerned about Hamlet's strange activities. So he sent for Rosencrantz and Guildenstern, two of Hamlet's old schoolfriends. He had a little job for them.

"I'm sure you've heard about Hamlet's – er – problem," Claudius began.

"We're so worried about him," added Queen Gertrude. "I mean, he's upset about his father dying, of course, but he's never behaved this oddly before."

"He really hasn't been himself recently," Claudius went on, "and, as friends of his, we were wondering if you could help us out. We'd like you to come and stay in the castle for a while. You could spend some time with him – and perhaps find out what the problem is. And then come back and tell me. Immediately."

❧

It broke Hamlet's heart to upset Ophelia, but he knew he couldn't tell her what was really going on. Only Horatio knew the truth. If anyone else found out, Hamlet's plans might make their way back to Claudius, and then he would never get his revenge.

But perhaps Hamlet would soon have a solution to his problem. Not long after his visit to Ophelia, a troupe of actors turned up at the castle, hoping to entertain the court with a performance. That was when Hamlet had a brilliant idea.

He asked the troupe to stage *The Murder of Gonzago*, a traditional story about the murder of a king. But he wrote a new version of the play for them to perform. In Hamlet's version, instead of being stabbed, King Gonzago had poison poured into his ear.

"As soon as I see the look on Claudius's face, I'll know if it's true," Hamlet said to Horatio as they watched the actors rehearsing. "You watch him carefully too. If he looks startled, we'll know he did it."

~~

Meanwhile, the king and queen and their advisors were discussing what could possibly be wrong with the prince.

"He's simply depressed, my lord," said Rosencrantz.

"His grief for his father has turned his head, your majesty," explained Guildenstern. "But I'm sure it's only temporary."

"No, no, no," interrupted Polonius. "It's lovesickness that's the problem. He loved Ophelia, but I told her to reject him, and now he's broken-hearted. It's all my fault."

Deep down, however, Claudius knew that none of these things was the problem. He began to suspect that Hamlet knew a little too much about what had happened to his father. And he was afraid of what the prince might do.

"I know," he announced brightly. "What Hamlet needs is some time away – some fresh air! A boat trip to England would be just the thing!"

"Of course!" said the queen, feeling relieved. "That will cure his unhappiness."

"And the players are performing for us tonight – I'm sure that will cheer everyone up!" said Claudius. "Then we can make arrangements for Hamlet to set off tomorrow. Rosencrantz and Guildenstern, you'll go with him to make sure he's safe."

As evening fell, the members of the court, in their best finery, assembled in the great hall for the performance. The king and queen sat at the front. Behind them sat Polonius and Ophelia, Rosencrantz and Guildenstern and all the other advisors and courtiers. Hamlet and Horatio positioned themselves to one side, so that they could see Claudius's face.

The lights in the hall were snuffed out, and the play began. Everyone knew *The Murder of Gonzago* and had seen it several times, but they watched politely as, on the stage, the king and queen declared their love for each other, the king fell asleep, and the king's evil nephew Lucianus came creeping up to murder him. But instead of wielding a knife, the actor playing Lucianus carried a small bottle.

Just as Hamlet had instructed, Lucianus carefully tipped the bottle, and poured a green liquid into the sleeping player-king's ear.

There was a kerfuffle in the front row. Claudius stood up shakily, clutching his head and groaning.

"The king is unwell," Ophelia cried out.

"Stop the play!" yelled Polonius.

"The lamps," wailed Claudius. "Light the lamps; I have to see my way."

"What's wrong, dear?" asked the queen. She bustled after Claudius as he stumbled from the room. Everyone else followed like a gaggle of geese, leaving Hamlet and Horatio alone with the dumbfounded actors.

"Did you see that!?" Hamlet exclaimed. "It couldn't have worked better!"

"I did!" said Horatio.

"The very second Lucianus poisoned the king…"

"It certainly seemed that way."

"Hamlet!" Polonius, the Lord Chamberlain, had returned. "The queen wishes to see you now!" he instructed.

"Alright, alright!" said Hamlet. "I'm going."

೨൭

Meanwhile, the terrified Claudius arranged an urgent meeting with Rosencrantz and Guildenstern. "I don't know what's wrong with Hamlet, but he's quite insane," he told them.

"He's a danger to the court. The three of you will set sail first thing in the morning. And you'll deliver this letter to the king of England."

"Of course, your majesty," said Rosencrantz, taking the sealed letter.

Polonius came in. "The prince has gone to see his mother," he said. "But perhaps someone else should be there, just in case he behaves unreasonably. I'll go to her room and hide behind the curtains."

"Good idea," Claudius said.

Then, when everyone had left, he took off his crown, fell to his knees, and clasped his hands together. But he could not bring himself to pray.

"How can I beg forgiveness," he cried, "when I'm still enjoying the rewards for what I did? The queen, the crown, this royal chamber – I don't deserve any of them. My crime is too evil to be forgiven – and now Hamlet knows! My only chance of survival is to get rid of him."

Hamlet had not gone directly to his mother's chamber. He had stopped on the way, thinking about what to do next. Now he knew for certain that Claudius was guilty, he should kill him at once. He clutched his dagger, ready to act.

His route took him past the king's chamber. Leaning around the door, he saw Claudius on his knees, his hands clasped. His eyes were closed, and there were tears on his cheeks.

"I should kill him," Hamlet told himself. "But he's praying – probably begging God for forgiveness. If I kill him now, he'll probably go to Heaven. That's no good! No, it'll have to wait." And so he walked on to his mother's chamber, and knocked on the door.

There was a scuffling noise inside. It was the queen pushing Polonius behind the curtains so that he could spy on Hamlet.

"Quick!" she said. "That'll be him!" Then she called out, "Come in, dear!"

Hamlet opened the door. "You asked to see me, mother?"

"Yes, Hamlet. I wanted to tell you that you deeply offended the king with that play."

"*I* offended the king!?" Hamlet shouted. "What about you, mother? What about what you did to the real king – my father, King Hamlet the first?"

"What are you talking about?"

"You know very well what I'm talking about."

"If you're going to insult me, I'll fetch the guards!" the QUEEN threatened.

"No!" said Hamlet. "There's no need for that. What you need to do is see yourself for what you are. A bad wife who betrayed her husband!" And he pushed her into the chair in front of her dressing table, so that she could see herself in the mirror.

"Get off me!" the QUEEN screamed. "Guards, he's attacking me! Help!"

Behind the curtain, Polonius thought Hamlet must be trying to murder the QUEEN. So he too called for help. "Help! Guards!" he shouted.

Hamlet spun around to see where the muffled male voice had come from. The king must have sneaked into the chamber. Now he was hiding behind the curtains – Hamlet could see them trembling where he stood! The creeping, cheating coward! Well, one thing was for sure – he wasn't praying now. Without a further thought, Hamlet drew his dagger and stabbed through the curtains into the QUAKING figure behind them.

"Hamlet! What have you done?" cried the QUEEN, as the body slumped to the floor.

"Simply avenging my father," said Hamlet. "Claudius killed a king, and so have I."

"Killed a king?" Gertrude said, puzzled.

Hamlet pulled at the curtain, and to his horror, saw that the body was Polonius.

∽∾

The next morning, Hamlet found himself on a ship to England.

As they had argued over Polonius's body, Hamlet had told his mother the truth. He knew she had been secretly in love with Claudius. He knew Claudius had murdered his father. And he intended to take revenge.

Gertrude had no choice. If she told everyone the truth, she would be admitting her own guilt. They all thought Hamlet was insane, so that was the best story to stick to.

So she said that Hamlet had seen a movement behind the curtains, gone beserk and attacked Polonius in a moment of insanity, and must be sent to England for the good of his health. She hardly dared think about what would happen when he returned.

107

But, as Hamlet was soon to discover, Claudius had done all he could to make sure that didn't happen.

As the ship sailed away from the Danish coast, Rosencrantz and Guildenstern went up on deck to sit in the sunshine. Hamlet stayed in the cabin. As he lay in his bunk, rocking to and fro, his eye fell on a letter that was poking out of Rosencrantz's bag.

After quickly checking that no one was coming, Hamlet pulled out the letter. It was addressed to the king of England. He unfolded it carefully.

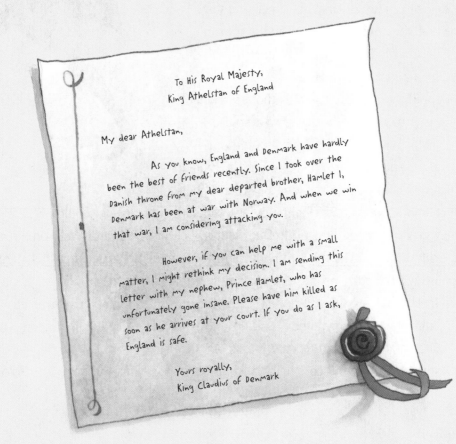

To His Royal Majesty,
King Athelstan of England

My dear Athelstan,

As you know, England and Denmark have hardly been the best of friends recently. Since I took over the Danish throne from my dear departed brother, Hamlet I, Denmark has been at war with Norway. And when we win that war, I am considering attacking you.

However, if you can help me with a small matter, I might rethink my decision. I am sending this letter with my nephew, Prince Hamlet, who has unfortunately gone insane. Please have him killed as soon as he arrives at your court. If you do as I ask, England is safe.

Yours royally,
King Claudius of Denmark

Hamlet quickly took a piece of parchment from his own belongings and rewrote the letter, replacing his own name with those of Rosencrantz and Guildenstern. He had just pushed the replacement letter into Rosencrantz's bag when he heard shouts from the deck.

"Pirates!" the lookout yelled. "Pirates ahoy! Take shelter below deck!"

As the other passengers crowded into their cabins, Hamlet gathered his belongings, along with the old letter, and ran up to the deck. The ship was sailing at full speed, but it wasn't fast enough, and the pirate ship was gaining on them. "Turn and attack!" the captain ordered, and the ship was steered around in order to ram the pirates as they approached. As the two boats crashed together, the side of the smaller pirate ship splintered and

cracked. It would have to return to shore.
Some of the sailors took out their swords
to keep the pirates from jumping aboard,
while the others steered the ship away. No
one noticed Hamlet leaping nimbly onto
the pirate ship and hiding under a spare sail.

Meanwhile, back in Denmark, the queen was wringing her hands with worry. Not
about Hamlet – she had no idea about Claudius's letter – but about Ophelia. The poor girl
had lost Hamlet's love, and now she had lost her dear father Polonius too. She had taken
to her bed, and was behaving very strangely. Gertrude sent a maidservant to check on her.

"How is she now?" the queen asked when the maid returned.

"Not well at all, madam," said the maid. "She keeps singing strange songs, and
whenever she speaks, mere flapdoodle comes out. She talks of her father, but she makes
no sense at all."

"Oh dear," the queen sighed, and went to tell her husband.

"Poor Ophelia," agreed Claudius. "It's the grief, of course. Her beloved father's
death, and..."

"What's that noise?" said the queen suddenly. There were shouts outside, and she
could hear the thumping of boots. A servant rushed into the room.

"Your majesties, it's Laertes, Ophelia's brother!" he panted. "He's come back from
France with an army. They've overpowered the guards!"

"Laertes!" The queen stood up, horrified. "What are we going to tell him?"

"He knows his father's dead, and he wants revenge!" said the servant.

But the king was calm. "Leave this to me," he said.

"WHAT HAPPENED TO MY FATHER!?" Laertes roared, as he stormed into the
room, his sword at the ready.

"Polonius was killed, Laertes," said Claudius. "I'm very sorry."

"But it wasn't our fault!" added Gertrude hurriedly.

"I'll get my revenge!" Laertes growled, stepping towards the king.

"Of course," said Claudius. "We're all grieving for poor Polonius."

Then they heard a girl's voice. They all turned around and saw Ophelia in the
doorway, dresssed in her white nightgown.

Her eyes were staring, her feet were bare, and she was carrying handfuls of wild flowers. She began to sing again, wandering towards them, her eyes rolling as she waved her arms this way and that.

Then she began handing out the flowers to everyone. "There's rosemary, for remembrance," she said to Laertes. "Pansies for you, which stand for thoughts," she said as she thrust more limp flowers into Queen Gertrude's hands. "And a daisy for the king!" she said, giving Claudius a single, drooping daisy.

Laertes had been calmed by the king's words, but as soon as he saw the state Ophelia was in, he was angry again. "What have you done to my sister?" he snarled, his hand moving to the hilt of his sword.

"Laertes, I know how upset you are, but we need to talk," said Claudius cunningly. "Let me explain. I promise you, we are as upset by all this as you are."

"Come on, dear," said the Queen, leading Ophelia away.

"You see, Laertes," Claudius soothed, when they had gone. "It was Hamlet that murdered your father. He's become very strange – almost insane."

"Then why send him to England?" Laertes demanded. "Why not just kill him?"

"Well," said the king, "firstly, his mother dotes on him. She couldn't bear it if I were to have him executed. And secondly, he's very popular with the people of Denmark. If I'd killed him myself, they would have hated me. So I sent him away instead. But don't worry, I've made sure – "

The king was interrupted by knocking, and a messenger entered with a letter.

"From Prince Hamlet, your majesty."

"From Hamlet?" The king went pale. He opened the letter and read it.

"Well? What does he say?" asked Laertes.

"He's coming back tomorrow!" said Claudius. "That's... not quite what I was expecting."

"Let him come," Laertes snarled. "I'll be waiting for him!"

"But we must do this carefully," said Claudius. "We must make it look like an accident. Listen. When he gets back, you'll challenge him to a duel. Not to the death – just a gentlemen's game. But you'll use a real sword, and 'accidentally' wound him."

"I'll dip my sword in poison," said Laertes. "So even if I only scratch him, he'll die."

"And to make extra sure, I'll prepare some special wine," the king said. "If the fight isn't going your way, I'll offer you both a drink to refresh yourselves. His will be poisoned."

"Perfect," said Laertes.

"Gentlemen..." The queen appeared in the doorway. She was white and trembling.

"What is it, my dear?"

"It's Ophelia. Laertes, I'm so sorry. Your sister has drowned."

Laertes stared at her, unbelieving.

"She escaped again," the queen went on, "and ran down to the river. She climbed the weeping willow tree, but the branch broke and she fell in. Her nightdress weighed her down and she was dragged beneath the water."

Laertes thought his heart would break. But, instead, it hardened. His father's murder, Ophelia's death – it was all Hamlet's fault. He would have his revenge tomorrow.

≈

The next day, a group of mourners carried Ophelia's body towards a distant corner of the chapel graveyard. There was no grand funeral. The priest had said that Ophelia had drowned herself deliberately, and must have an unmarked grave.

Laertes stared helplessly at his poor sister as she was lowered into the ground. Then, just as the gravediggers reached for their shovels, he burst into tears and jumped down into the grave alongside her. "Wait! Just let me say goodbye!" he wailed, taking the body in his arms.

"What's going on here?"

They all turned at the sound of the familiar voice, and were amazed to see Hamlet approaching the grave.

"Hamlet!" cried the queen. "He's back! Oh my darling son – it's Ophelia..."

Hamlet looked into the grave and saw Ophelia's limp body, and Laertes glaring up at him. Laertes gently laid the body down, then scrambled out of the grave and grabbed Hamlet by the throat.

"You!" he snarled. "You killed my father – and now my dear sister too!"

"Me?" choked Hamlet, prising Laertes's fingers from his neck. "I loved Ophelia. I loved her more than a brother ever could."

"How dare you!?" Laertes yelled. He flung himself at Hamlet, and the two of them rolled around by the grave, each trying to hold the other off while reaching for his dagger.

"No! Stop them!" squealed Gertrude.

"Separate them!" Claudius shouted, and the courtiers pulled the two men apart. "We'll finish this burial with dignity!" the king snapped. "Then we'll go inside and settle this argument the civilized way – with a gentlemanly duel."

In the great hall, Hamlet and Laertes stood facing each other. Each held a long, narrow fencing foil. But Laertes and Claudius knew that only Hamlet's foil was the blunt kind, used for harmless duels. The foil in Laertes's hand was sharp – and wet with deadly poison.

Hamlet had been ready to kill Claudius as soon as he returned. Now he was involved in this absurd duel.

"There's really no need for this," he said to Laertes. "Your father's death was an accident, and I'm sorry. As for Ophelia, I'm just as upset as you are."

"We'll let the duel decide who's more upset," said Laertes, trembling with rage.

"Ready to start?" said Claudius cheerily, arranging cups of wine on a side table. "Let the duel begin!"

Everyone fell silent as Hamlet and Laertes began to circle around each other. Hamlet was a well-trained fighter, and he fenced well. His flashing blade drove Laertes back across the hall as the two foils clashed again and again. He slashed and pointed, dodged and dived, until Laertes was exhausted. Finally, Hamlet managed to touch his opponent's waistcoat with the tip of his blunt blade.

"A hit!" cried Osrick, the courtier who was acting as an umpire. "Hamlet scores!"

"Play again!" the king called from his throne, pretending to enjoy the game.

But the same thing happened again. Hamlet was too good for Laertes. He forced him back, parrying and blocking so that Laertes's foil could never touch him, and scored a second hit.

"Hamlet's winning!" said the queen excitedly. "Let's drink to him!" She picked up a cup of wine from the side table. Claudius reached towards her urgently. "No!" he hissed.

Hamlet turned his head for a second to see what was happening. But, just at that moment, Laertes leapt towards him. Hamlet was caught off guard, and felt his arm scratched with the sharp foil. The shock of the cut made him lash out at Laertes with his own foil, and both swords clattered to the ground. Hamlet grabbed the nearest one, and carried on fighting. He saw a look of terror replace the anger in his enemy's eyes as he slashed forward. He soon scored a third hit. But to his surprise, the foil sliced through Laertes's shirt, and his shoulder began to bleed. The blade must have been sharper than he thought.

"No...!" Laertes dropped to his knees, clutching his wound. "I am slain!"

"It's just a cut," laughed Osrick. "Hamlet has won the duel."

But Hamlet had rushed to his mother's side. She had fallen to the floor.

"She's fainted because of the blood," Osrick explained.

But Gertrude was choking. "No, I am poisoned," she gasped. "Hamlet... the wine..." Then, with a last, strangled groan, she fell back, and her eyes closed.

Hamlet turned back to face the room, his eyes narrow with suspicion.

"Someone is plotting here," he said. "Lock all the doors. We must find the villain."

"It's too late," said Laertes, pointing at the foil in Hamlet's hand. "Hamlet, that sword is poisoned. We both have our death wounds. This plotting is the king's work."

"Poisoned...?" Hamlet brought the sword up to his face, peering at its bloodstained tip. He felt the scratch on his arm begin to tingle. Looking beyond the sword, he saw Claudius staring at him helplessly.

"Then let it work once more!" Hamlet cried. He strode forward and thrust the sword into Claudius's stomach.

"Help! Treason!" gasped the king, but no one moved.

Then Hamlet took the cup and pushed his uncle's head back against his throne, so that his crown clattered to the floor. Holding Claudius's mouth open, he poured the poisoned wine across his face. "Go where you belong, uncle," he said, as Claudius slumped from the throne and collapsed onto the ground.

"Hamlet," Laertes whispered weakly, dragging himself nearer. "Please let us forgive each other, before we die." And he grabbed Hamlet's hand, before collapsing himself.

Hamlet's wound was smaller, but the poison was starting to work. He looked around at the bodies of his mother and uncle, and at poor Laertes before him. He thought of Polonius, Ophelia, and his dear father in their graves. He had avenged his father at last.

As his vision began to blur, he saw Horatio step forward and pick up the wine goblet from beside Claudius's body.

"There's a drop left," Horatio said, sadly. "I'd rather go with all of you, than be left alone in this ruined country."

"No!" cried Hamlet, finding just enough strength to lunge forward and grab the cup from his friend. He fell back onto the steps leading to the throne, and drained the last drop himself. "Horatio, you must live to tell this terrible tale."

"The Norwegians are coming!" a messenger called from outside the hall. "They're going to take over the castle!"

"Surrender the Danish throne to Norway," whispered Hamlet. And with that, his head dropped to the ground, and he died.

# The Merchant of Venice

Antonio was a merchant in the great city of Venice in Italy. His three trading ships were constantly sailing around the world, carrying cargoes of silk, spices and precious stones.

One warm afternoon in spring, Antonio was sitting outside a tavern with his friends Bassanio, Gratiano, Lorenzo and Salerio. They were all laughing and joking, but Antonio seemed anxious.

"What's the matter, Antonio?" Salerio asked. "Worrying about your ships again?"

"Well, if I had three ships all out trading at the same time, full of such valuable cargo, I'd probably worry too," said Gratiano.

Soon, Salerio, Lorenzo and Gratiano said farewell, leaving Antonio with his best friend, Bassanio. Antonio didn't want to think about his ships, so he changed the subject.

"Now, Bassanio," he smiled. "How are things going with that lady from Belmont?"

"You mean Portia!" said Bassanio. "Oh Antonio, I'm so in love with her, and I'd like to go back to Belmont to ask her to marry me. But I've run out of money. I know you've already lent me some, but I was wondering if I could have a little more. Then, if I do marry Portia, I'll be very rich, and I'll be able to pay you back. I need three thousand ducats."

"I would if I could," Antonio sighed, "but all my wealth is in my ships and cargo. Until they return, I'm as poor as you are. You'll have to borrow from someone else."

"Like who?"

"Like Shylock, I suppose," said Antonio.

Shylock was a Jewish money-lender who lived in Venice. Antonio and his friends, who were Christians, did not like him. Everyone knew he had plenty of money to lend, but he charged high interest. If you took a loan from him, you had to pay back much more than you had borrowed.

"I'll tell you what," said Antonio. "My ships are due back in two months. Ask Shylock for a three-month loan, and then when my ships come in I'll be able to pay him back for you. Then you'll owe me the money instead of him, and I won't charge interest."

Bassanio thanked his friend heartily, and went to find Shylock.

"Well, well," said Shylock, when he heard Bassanio's request. "Three thousand ducats, eh?"

"Yes – and I need the loan for three months," said Bassanio.

"Three months! Well, well," Shylock mused, twirling his moustache.

"Please, Shylock. Antonio will guarantee the loan. His ships are back in two months, and he'll pay you back then. I know you and he aren't the best of friends, but you can trust him."

"Ships?" said Shylock, suspiciously. "Ships are only made of planks, and sailors are only human. What about pirates, and storms, and mutinies? How do I know his ships will come back safely? I need to speak to him."

"Of course," said Bassanio, trying to be as friendly as he could. "We are all having dinner at his house tonight. Why don't you come along?"

At that moment, Antonio appeared. "I thought I should come and make it clear that I will pay off Bassanio's loan," he said.

"Ah, it's the wonderful Antonio," said Shylock sarcastically. "The same Antonio who has so often insulted me in the market square. The same Antonio who just last week called me a Jewish dog, and spat on my cloak. So, you think a dog can lend three thousand ducats, do you?"

"I know you can," said Antonio. "As for me insulting you, well, I'm sorry, but we have always been enemies. In fact, you should be happy to lend money to an enemy. That way, you won't feel bad about charging all that interest."

"I would have been your friend, if you'd ever let me," said Shylock. "I never called *you* names. I would be happy to make this a friendly arrangement. Bassanio has very kindly invited me to dinner at your house, and I'm prepared to make this an interest-free loan."

But Antonio couldn't forget how much he hated Shylock, and he did not thank him for his offer. This made Shylock angry.

"Very well," he said at last. "I won't charge interest, but I will set a bond. If my three thousand ducats are not repaid three months today, at midday, Antonio must give me a pound of his flesh, to be taken from his body wherever I choose."

"It's a deal," said Antonio, glaring at Shylock.

"No!" Bassanio interrupted. "That's horrible! I'll just go without the money."

"Don't worry, Bassanio," Antonio said. "The date for repayment is three months away, and my ships are back in two months. I will repay the loan. Everything will be fine."

Still scowling at each other, Shylock and Antonio shook hands on the deal, and Shylock agreed to come to dinner that night with an agreement for Antonio to sign.

Meanwhile, in Belmont, a beautiful city several days' sail from Venice, Portia was sitting in her house, complaining to her lady-in-waiting, Nerissa.

"It's ridiculous!" she said crossly. "My father's will is making it impossible for me to get married."

Portia's father had died the year before, leaving her a huge fortune. But he had been terrified that, since Portia would be so rich, she would be plagued by men who only wanted her for her money.

So, in his will, he had left instructions that any man who wanted to marry his daughter must choose from three caskets – one made of gold, one made of silver, and one made of lead. One of the caskets contained a portrait of Portia, and whoever chose it could marry her – as long as she agreed. However, the rules also said that anyone who made the wrong choice must swear never to marry at all. Not surprisingly, this put off most of the men who came to woo her.

Nerissa teased Portia about her moaning. "Poor old Portia," she laughed. "You're the richest lady in Belmont, you have a fine house, and you're beautiful too. It's such a hard life."

Portia smiled. "You're right, I am lucky, and I shouldn't complain," she said. "It's nice to have money. But love is more important. That's what I really want."

"So," Nerissa giggled, "do you mean you didn't like any of the fine gentlemen who've turned up recently?"

"No, I did not!" said Portia. "They were all useless! First there was the Prince of Naples, who did nothing but talk about his horse! Then the Count of Palatine, who I swear is the dullest man on Earth. And Monsieur Le Bon from France, who can't stop playing practical jokes. As for the Englishman and the Scotsman – when they started having a fight I didn't know where to look!"

Nerissa laughed until the tears rolled down her cheeks. "You must like *someone*!" she exclaimed.

"Well... there is one man I like," said Portia. "His name's Bassanio – do you remember him? The last time he was here was before my father died – but I liked him very much. I wish he would come back."

Just then, a servant came in to announce that a new suitor had arrived.

"It's the Prince of Morocco, madam," he said, showing in a tall, good-looking gentleman wearing a jewel-encrusted suit.

"Your ladyship," the newcomer said politely. "I have always admired your beauty, and I have heard about the test set by your father. I would like to offer myself as your future husband."

Portia looked him up and down. He was very handsome. "Well, it's for the caskets to decide, not me," she said, "and you're welcome to try your hand at them. But you do know the rules, don't you? If you don't succeed, you must never marry anyone."

"I accept the challenge," said the prince. "I will make my choice tomorrow."

~~

Back in Venice, Shylock's daughter, Jessica, was making plans. For several months, she had been in love with Lorenzo, one of Antonio's friends. But Lorenzo was a Christian, and Jessica knew Shylock would never allow them to marry. So she and Lorenzo were planning to run away.

*My darling Lorenzo,*
*Tonight is our chance to run away together.*
*My father is going to dinner at Antonio's house, and I will be left alone. To avoid suspicion, I will disguise myself as a boy, and wait for you to collect me. Then we can leave Venice before he finds out I'm gone.*
*Your loving sweetheart,*
*Jessica*

When she heard that her father would be going to Antonio's house for dinner that night, she quickly wrote a letter, sealed it and gave it to a messenger to deliver. "I need you to take this to Lorenzo before tonight," she said. "And don't say a word about it to my father."

When he read the letter, Lorenzo kissed it, and clutched it to his heart. Then he went to find Gratiano to ask for his help. He knew Gratiano was planning to travel to Belmont with Bassanio – they were to set sail that night, after Antonio's dinner party. Lorenzo realized that the safest way for Jessica and himself to escape would be to go to Belmont with them.

~~

Shylock was almost ready to set off for Antonio's house. Into his bag he put the three thousand ducats, and the loan agreement, ready for Antonio to sign. Then he went to talk to Jessica.

"Here are the house keys," he said. "I should be back from this tiresome dinner party by midnight. And I don't want you going out to any parties. Make sure you stay indoors."

"Yes, father," said Jessica, trying to sound as sweet and obedient as she could. But as soon as Shylock had set off, she ran to her room and packed her things. Then she changed into a set of boys' clothes she had borrowed from one of the servants, and waited at the window for Lorenzo.

119

Considering he was having his oldest enemy to dinner, Antonio
thought the evening was going very well. He had signed Shylock's agreement,
Shylock had handed the money to Bassanio, and everyone was enjoying the meal.

　　After the main course, Gratiano stood up.

　　"I'm so sorry to have to leave early," he explained, "but I'm going to Belmont with
Bassanio tonight, and I have to go home and pack. Thank you for a delicious dinner,
Antonio. Bassanio, I'll meet you at the docks at midnight."

　　"I'll come with you for some fresh air before I go home to bed," said Lorenzo,
leaving his seat. "I'm quite tired, actually," he added, with an obvious yawn.

But, as soon as Gratiano and Lorenzo were
outside, they headed straight for Shylock's house, where they
collected Jessica. With her pretending to be their manservant, they ran down to
the docks, and waited for Bassanio. At midnight he arrived, and they all boarded a ship
bound for Belmont.

When Shylock went home that night, the house was quiet, and he assumed Jessica was
asleep in bed. He did not discover she was missing until the next morning. As soon as he
realized she was gone, he ran out into the street.

"My daughter! My daughter! Where is she!?" he yelled at anyone who would listen.
Then he stormed back to Antonio's house and thumped on the door.

"My daughter is missing!" he roared, when a bleary-eyed Antonio appeared.
"I know this has something to do with you and your good-for-nothing friends! It's that
Lorenzo, isn't it! He's the one who's been hanging around her! Tell me where they are!"

"I swear I don't know!" said Antonio, truthfully. "They're not here..."

"They must have run away to Belmont with Bassanio and Gratiano! That's right,
isn't it?" Shylock shouted.

"I don't know anything about it," Antonio repeated, but he was worried. If Bassanio had helped Jessica and Lorenzo to run away to Belmont, and Shylock found out, there would be big trouble.

So, to put Shylock off, he said: "Actually, they've probably gone to Genoa. I'm sure I heard Lorenzo say something about going to Genoa soon."

Shylock turned around and stomped home in a furious rage.

"I don't believe him," he mumbled to himself. "I have been tricked. Antonio and his friends have got my money, and now they've taken my daughter too. I will make Antonio pay for this! If his repayment is even a day late, I will have my bond – I'll take that pound of flesh from him. I'll take it even if he's a minute late! I'll make him suffer!"

~~

In Belmont, the Prince of Morocco was ready to make his choice. Portia showed him into the room where the caskets were kept. Each casket was inscribed with a cryptic message.

On the gold casket were the words: *Who chooseth me, shall gain what many men desire.*
The silver casket declared: *Who chooseth me, shall get as much as he deserves.*
The words on the lead casket read: *Who chooseth me, must give everything he has.*

The prince thought long and hard. Finally, he said: "Well, many men desire Portia. That must be what the inscription on the gold casket means. And since she's such a wealthy lady, her portrait must be in the most valuable box. I'll choose the gold one."

He opened the gold casket. Inside, to his horror, he found a human skull. In its eye-socket was a rolled up piece of paper. The prince opened it out and read:

*All that glistens is not gold:*
*Often have you heard that told.*
*You weren't as wise as you were bold,*
*And all alone you shall grow old.*

The poor Moroccan prince was bitterly disappointed, and left at once. But he had hardly been gone an hour when another suitor arrived. This time, it was the Prince of Aragon.

"I'm so delighted to be here!" he announced excitedly. "And I'm ready to make my choice of the caskets! I know all the rules!"

Portia rolled her eyes wearily. "Come on," she said. "I'll show you where they are."

The Prince of Aragon was immediately drawn to the silver casket.

"Why, silver is what money is made of," he said. "It must stand for Portia's riches. As for the gold casket, I don't want '*what many men desire*'. No, I deserve Portia, and the silver casket says if I choose it, I'll get what I deserve! That's the one!"

He opened the silver casket, to be faced with a picture of a fool. Pinned to it was another piece of paper with a message on it:

*If the box you chose was this,*
*You have made your choice amiss.*
*You shall never Portia kiss,*
*Nor live your life in wedded bliss.*

The Prince of Aragon left in a very bad mood indeed.

"Oh dear," Portia sighed to Nerissa after he had gone. "What idiots all these men are. My father was right — they're all obsessed with my money."

"At least now we know which is the right casket," said Nerissa.

"Yes, but my father's will says I can't give any suitor the answer."

"Perhaps Bassanio will come back soon, and try choosing a casket," said Nerissa.

"I wish he would," Portia sighed. And her wish was soon granted. A few days later, Bassanio arrived in Belmont with his friends. When she saw him, Portia could barely conceal her delight. She explained to him all about the caskets, and longed to tell him the right answer. But she knew she must not. Instead, she begged him to take his time. "Wait a while, and spend some time with me," she said. "You and Gratiano must visit us every day — we'll go for walks, and have picnics, and enjoy the summer."

The truth was, Portia was afraid Bassanio would choose the wrong casket — and if he did, she would never see him again. So, for two months, Bassanio visited her every day. And, as the weeks went by, the two of them fell more and more deeply in love.

Meanwhile, Shylock had sent a friend named Tubal to Genoa to look for Jessica. But when Tubal came back, he said no one in Genoa had seen Lorenzo and Jessica at all.

"Now I'm *sure* Antonio tricked me," Shylock fumed, angrier than ever.

Just then, Antonio's friend Salerio arrived. "What do you want?" Shylock snapped.

"I have news," said Salerio, looking miserable. "Antonio's been waiting for his ships to come in, but they haven't turned up. They're lost at sea. He can't pay you back."

Shylock would normally have been upset by this, but he could hardly hide his glee.

"So," he smirked. "Antonio will have to give me that pound of flesh, after all."

"Please, Shylock, don't ask him for the pound of flesh," Salerio begged. "It's cruel."

"Cruel?" Shylock shouted. "*Cruel*!? Hasn't he been cruel to me? Scorning me in public, just for being Jewish? Thinking he can trick me, and lie to me, and spit on me, just because I'm Jewish? Calling me a dog – an animal – because I'm Jewish? Jews are human, you know. Don't Jews have eyes, and hands, and organs, just as Christians do? Don't Jews have feelings? If you prick us, don't we bleed? If you tickle us, don't we laugh? And if you do us wrong, don't we deserve revenge? That's all I want, Salerio – my revenge. Antonio has signed an agreement to say he'll give me a pound of flesh, and I'm going to take it."

As time went on, Bassanio began to worry about Antonio's ships. He hoped they had returned safely, and that Antonio had been able to pay Shylock, but until he went back to Venice, he couldn't be sure. So he told Portia he must go to Venice soon, and he wanted to choose from the caskets before he left. She begged him to wait, but his mind was made up.

When he saw the caskets and their inscriptions, Bassanio considered them carefully.

"The gold one can't be right," he said to himself. "*What many men desire* must mean gold itself, and although I'd like to be richer, that's not why I love her."

He turned to the silver casket. "*Who chooseth me, shall get as much as he deserves*," he read. "Well I certainly don't deserve Portia! I love her, but I'm hardly worthy of her!"

Standing watching him, Portia smiled to herself.

"That leaves the lead casket," said Bassanio. "It says: *Who chooseth me, must give everything he has*. Well, of course, if I marry Portia, I will give her everything I have – though I don't have much to give! Well, here goes." He opened the lead casket.

He gasped when he saw the beautiful picture of Portia inside. He picked up the piece of paper attached to it, and read:

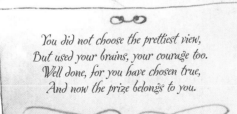

*You did not choose the prettiest view,*
*But used your brains, your courage too.*
*Well done, for you have chosen true,*
*And now the prize belongs to you.*

124

"It's the right one!" he said delightedly. "Oh Portia, will you marry me?"

"Yes, yes, yes!" Portia cried, flinging her arms around him. "And you *are* worthy of me, Bassanio – you are the only one who is, because you love me, and not my money. That's what my father wanted. And now I can see how wise he was, and I'm so grateful to him! Now I can get married, and to a man I love! Let's make the arrangements for the wedding at once!"

Overhearing them, Gratiano and Nerissa came into the room.

"We're getting married!" Portia cried, and Nerissa hugged her, while Gratiano congratulated Bassanio. Then Gratiano said, "Actually, we have an announcement to make as well. While you've been courting, we've fallen in love ourselves. I've asked Nerissa to marry me!"

"Why, this is everything I could wish for!" Portia said. "We'll both have husbands!"

"And Lorenzo and Jessica are planning to marry too," said Bassanio.

"We'll have a great big wedding party," said Portia, "and all get married together!"

But just then, Lorenzo and Jessica arrived with Antonio's friend Salerio, who had just come from Venice. "Bassanio," he said. "I have a letter from Antonio. I'm afraid it's not good news."

Bassanio read the letter. "This is terrible!" he said. "Antonio's ships are lost."

"What are you talking about?" Portia asked.

"Oh, Portia, I'm so sorry," Bassanio said. "I told you I was penniless, but that's not the whole truth. In fact, I am in debt to Shylock, Jessica's father. Antonio was going to pay the debt for me, but now he's ruined. The worst part is, he has promised that if he can't pay the debt, he'll give Shylock a pound of flesh. And Shylock is planning to take it."

"Who is this Antonio?" Portia asked.

"A merchant of Venice, and my oldest and dearest friend," said Bassanio, "He guaranteed this loan for me so that I could come here and woo you."

"The date for repayment draws near," said Salerio. "It is only days away."

"Right," said Portia, "the next ship to Venice sails this evening. We will get married at once, and have the party later. Bassanio, I will give you six thousand ducats to pay off the loan, and you must take it to Venice. If you leave tonight, you might make it in time."

And so a priest was called, and the weddings were held in a hurry. Portia and Nerissa gave Bassanio and Gratiano wedding rings to remind them that they were married.

"If you love us, you must promise never to take them off," Portia instructed. Bassanio and Gratiano promised not to take the rings off, kissed their wives, and set off for Venice with Salerio, taking the six thousand ducats with them.

But little did they know that Portia had no intention of staying behind.

"Nerissa, pack your bags," she said, as soon as they had gone. "We're going to Venice too. We'll see our husbands before they see us!"

"Why won't they see us?" asked Nerissa.

"Because we'll be in disguise! I'll pretend to be a young lawyer, and you will be my assistant. I know a real lawyer, Dr. Bellario, who will lend us lawyers' clothes and give me a letter of recommendation. If they don't make it in time, I have a plan to save Antonio."

On the day the debt was due, Antonio awoke with a chill in his heart. There was still no sign of Salerio, nor any word from Bassanio. In fact, they were hurrying back from Belmont as fast as they could, but their ship was delayed. They were going to be late.

When midday arrived, Shylock had Antonio arrested and taken to court, where he planned to put him on trial before the duke of Venice. He would show the court the agreement Antonio had signed, and claim his pound of flesh there and then. But just as the trial was about to begin, Bassanio, Gratiano and Salerio rushed in.

"We have the money!" Bassanio shouted. "Set the prisoner free."

"The time for repayment has passed," said Shylock. "Now I want my bond."

"Here's six thousand ducats," said Bassanio. "Twice the debt. Just let Antonio go."

"No," said Shylock. The date has passed, and I want my bond."

"I'll take Antonio's place," Bassanio offered. "Have a pound of my flesh instead."

"*No!*" yelled Shylock. "The deal says it's Antonio who has to give his flesh."

The duke intervened. "I'm afraid I can't stop Shylock from going ahead," he said. "Antonio did sign the agreement, so the law's on Shylock's side."

Shylock was just about to draw his knife, when the door opened and everyone turned around. They saw two strange young men walk in.

"Greetings," said one of them, in a high, squeaky voice. "I am Dr. Balthazar, a student of law, and this is my assistant. We have a letter from Dr. Bellario, the famous lawyer. He's heard about this case, and he's sent us to provide legal advice."

"You can say what you like," said Shylock, "but I will have my bond. I want to make Antonio suffer for what he's done to me, and I have a right to. This agreement says so."

"It's true," said the young stranger. "You are entitled to whatever the agreement says. But just let me see that agreement first. I'll check it for you." Shylock handed it over.

"Ah yes," said Dr. Balthazar. "A pound of flesh. Where are you going to take it from?"

"From his chest, next to his heart," said Shylock. Everyone stared at him in horror.

"You want Antonio to die!" Bassanio accused him.

"I want my pound of flesh," said Shylock innocently.

"Well, merchant," said Dr. Balthazar, "you'd better take off your shirt. Are you ready?"

"I am ready," Antonio replied. "Bassanio, Gratiano, Salerio, give me your hands. I will say farewell now, in case I die."

"Oh, my dear friend," said Bassanio, tears filling his eyes. "How could it have come to this? Thanks to you, I have a wonderful new wife, who is dearer to me than life itself — yet I would give her up in an instant if it meant I could help you."

"It's just as well your wife didn't hear you say that," Dr. Balthazar remarked, before continuing: "Shylock, you may now take your pound of flesh."

Shylock stepped forward, his knife in his hand.

"But do make sure," the young lawyer added, "that you don't take any blood, won't you? For in this agreement I see no mention of blood. Indeed, if you take so much as a drop of blood, why, you'll be put on trial yourself."

Shylock stopped in his tracks. "Well, go on," Dr. Balthazar urged him.

"Erm..." Shylock faltered. "I... I think I'll take the money after all."

"You've refused the money," said the lawyer, "so it's too late for that. All you can have is a pound of flesh. Don't you want it?"

Shylock threw his knife to the floor. "You have defeated me, Balthazar!" he growled. "I will take nothing. I have no choice."

"Oh, but wait a second," the lawyer said. "There's one more thing. Didn't you know that plotting to take another person's life is a serious crime? The punishment is to have your lands and your riches split in two. One half goes to your victim, the other half to the city of Venice. As for your life, it is at the mercy of the duke."

Trembling in horror, Shylock turned to the duke.

"I'll spare your life," said the duke kindly. "You will give half your wealth to Antonio, but instead of giving the other half to Venice, you'll just pay a fine. Antonio, do you agree?"

Antonio stood up, looking very relieved. "I have been Shylock's enemy, and I do not deserve half his wealth," he said. "Instead, I think it should go to his daughter Jessica. And Shylock must forgive her, and accept Lorenzo as his son-in-law. Then I'll be satisfied."

"Excellent," said the duke. "Clerk of the court, arrange for Shylock to pay the fine and to sign over half his wealth to his daughter." The court clerk led Shylock away.

Bassanio turned to the strange lawyer. "Good sir," he said, "we are eternally grateful for your help. Let me give you these six thousand ducats to say thank you."

"I don't need money," Dr. Balthazar said. "I'm happy to help. It was my pleasure."

"We must give you something," said Bassanio. "Isn't there anything you'd like?"

"Well, I do like that ring," the lawyer said, looking at Bassanio's hand. "I'll have that."

Bassanio looked anxious. "My ring?" he said. "Oh, I couldn't – it's just a cheap one."

"But I've really taken a fancy to it," Dr. Balthazar replied. "Honestly, that's all I want – if you really are grateful to me, of course."

Bassanio sighed. "Of course I am," he said, and gave Dr. Balthazar his ring.

"What a fine ring!" said the lawyer's assistant. "I would like one too."

"Your friend shall give his ring to my assistant," Dr. Balthazar said. "Then we'll consider ourselves well paid." Poor Gratiano was forced to hand over his ring as well.

❧

A few days later, Bassanio and Gratiano arrived in Belmont, bringing Antonio to meet their new wives. They found Portia and Nerissa waiting for them in Portia's garden, along with Lorenzo and Jessica. Bassanio told his wife all about what had happened in Venice, and gave her back her money. Antonio congratulated everyone on their recent weddings. All was well, until Nerissa suddenly said: "Gratiano? Where is the ring I gave you?"

"Ah..." said Gratiano. "You see, we had to give our rings to the lawyer and his assistant. It was all they would accept as payment..."

"You gave away your ring too!!!" Portia exclaimed to Bassanio.

"You don't understand!" protested Bassanio. "I tried to give him money – I promised him anything he wanted – but he asked for our rings."

"A likely story!" Portia said. "You gave that ring to some beautiful lady in Venice."

"That sounds more realistic," agreed Nerissa. "You've been wooing other women."

"I swear we haven't!" Bassanio pleaded. "We gave our rings to the lawyers!"

"It's true," said Antonio. "I saw it happen – they had no choice."

"Well," said Portia, "I suppose I'd better give you another ring, and Nerissa, you must give Gratiano one too. This time, you must *really* promise not to give them away!"

They both took out rings, and put them on their husbands' fingers.

Bassanio stared at his hand. "Why, this is the same ring!" he said.

"So is mine!" said Gratiano.

"Want to know where we got them from?" grinned Portia, while Nerissa started to giggle. "We came to Venice. We were at the court! I was Dr. Balthazar!"

"You!" gasped Bassanio. "It was *you*!?"

"And I was his assistant!" Nerissa laughed.

"You saved Antonio's life!" cried Bassanio. "Why, I have the cleverest wife in Belmont!"

"And there's more news," said Portia. "On our way back here, we heard that one of Antonio's ships has returned after all. It's slightly damaged, but the cargo is safe."

"I am not ruined!" cried Antonio delightedly. "I can still be a merchant of Venice!"

"And of course," said Portia, "there's news for Jessica too. Your father is to give you half his estate, and forgive you. You can return to Venice with your husband!"

And with that, the friends all went inside Portia's house, and celebrated their new-found happiness by eating, drinking, singing and dancing until dawn.

# As You Like It

"And so my father, on his deathbed, decided to leave everything to Oliver," Orlando explained, as he and Adam, an old manservant, were walking through the orchard. "He told Oliver to make sure he looked after me and Jake. He takes care of Jake, of course," Orlando said, "for they were always the best of friends. But I'm the youngest, and Oliver hates me. I know he wishes I had never been born. He gives me no money, he won't let me go to school – he won't even let me eat at the table with him. My father would turn in his grave if he could see what's happening."

"He would indeed, sir," said Adam. "Your father was a good master. And I'm afraid I can't say the same for your brother."

"Shhh – Oliver's coming," said Orlando. "Hide behind that big chestnut tree, and you'll see the way he treats me."

"What are you doing here, Orlando?" Oliver demanded.

"Just wasting time in the orchard," Orlando replied. "I've nothing much else to do."

"*The* orchard? I think you mean *my* orchard," said Oliver smugly. "Father left it to *me*."

"Oh, yes, I was forgetting," said Orlando sarcastically. "I beg your humble pardon, my lord. Of course I meant *your* orchard."

"How dare you mock me!" yelled Oliver, striking him across the face. But Orlando was stronger than his brother, and he retaliated by wrestling Oliver to the ground, then holding his neck in an armlock.

"Let me *go*!" Oliver gurgled.

"Boys, dear boys, please stop this," pleaded Adam, emerging from behind the tree.

"I'll let you go if you'll start treating me like a brother," Orlando told his brother. "Let me go to school, and give me a proper allowance. Or just give me my share of the money, and then I'll leave you in peace."

"Very well then, I will," panted Oliver, and Orlando released him. "I'll give you your share of the inheritance, if you promise you'll go away and never come back. Now get out of my sight. We'll sort it out tomorrow, after the wrestling match."

When Orlando had gone, Oliver went to find Charles, prizefighter at the court of Duke Frederick. A wrestling tournament was taking place there, and the next day, Orlando was due to fight Charles.

"It's about my little brother, Orlando," Oliver began. "You're to fight him in the tournament tomorrow."

"Yes," said Charles, "I've been worrying about it myself. I fear he's too young – he's probably too weak for me, and he could get hurt. Perhaps we should call it off."

"No, no, far from it!" said Oliver. "I've simply come to let you know what a devious little trickster he is. If you're not careful, he'll cheat, or trip you up – he could even have a knife hidden in his belt. Your wisest strategy is to beat him senseless as soon as you can. You may end up killing him, but I'm afraid it's the only way. I wanted to warn you."

Charles looked surprised, but he thanked Oliver and went on his way.

"Excellent," smirked Oliver, rubbing his hands together. "With any luck, that fight will be the end of Orlando – and then I won't have to pay him anything at all!"

Duke Frederick, who was holding the wrestling tournament at his palace, was not the real duke at all. The real duke was his brother, Duke Senior. A few months before, Frederick had forced Duke Senior out of power, and banished him from the court. His most loyal friends had gone with him and, according to local gossip, they were living in the nearby Forest of Arden. Only his daughter, Rosalind, had been allowed to stay behind, as she was best friends with Frederick's own daughter, Celia.

The next morning, Celia and Rosalind were walking in the palace gardens.

"Dear Rosalind, please cheer up," said Celia. "I'm so sorry about what happened."

"I miss my father," said Rosalind. "I can't stop thinking about him."

"There's nothing we can do about it now," Celia said, "but one day my father will die, and as I'm his only child, he'll leave everything to me. And then I will give it all back to you, I promise, or to your father if he is still living."

"Thank you, Celia," said Rosalind, squeezing her cousin's hand.

"Ladies!" called a silly, singsong voice, "Oh, ladies! You're going to miss all the fun!"

It was Touchstone, Duke Frederick's jester.

"What fun?" asked Rosalind.

"The wrestling, of course!" Touchstone cried, dancing around them. "It's about to start! You didn't see it yesterday, did you? Three men broke their ribs! It was very exciting."

"Hmmm, it sounds lovely," mumbled Rosalind, but Celia pulled her by the arm.

"Oh please, Rosalind, let's go and watch," she said. "It might cheer you up!"

As they arrived, Duke Frederick was taking his seat, and Orlando and Charles were preparing to fight.

"Is that boy going to wrestle Charles?" Rosalind gasped when she saw Orlando. "Oh, the poor thing! He'll never win!"

"Young man!" called Celia, and Orlando bowed to her. "This is too great a challenge," she told him. "You don't have to fight Charles – you can back out."

"I want to fight him," said Orlando. "I have nothing to lose. And if I am killed, why, few will miss me."

"Then I wish you strength, and good luck," Rosalind said, gazing at him in admiration.

The fight began, and at first the girls hid their faces, afraid to see Orlando getting hurt. But, to everyone's surprise, the match went the other way. Orlando was surprisingly strong. After skipping around Charles for a while, he managed to grab him and throw him to the ground. When Charles could not get up, Orlando was declared the winner.

"What is your name, young man?" Duke Frederick called, as Charles was carried away on a stretcher.

"I am Orlando, son of Sir Rowland de Boys," Orlando announced.

The duke's face fell. "Sir Rowland de Boys, eh?" he said. "One of my arch enemies." And he stood up and walked away, with a scowl on his face.

But Rosalind stepped in. "My father was a friend of Sir Rowland," she said, "and I will reward this fighter, as the duke should have done." And she went over and gave Orlando her gold necklace as a prize. "Well done," she said, smiling at him.

Celia was calling her, but Rosalind lingered to stare just a little longer at the handsome young man, who was obviously so much stronger and braver than she had at first thought. And he really was very good-looking indeed.

As for Orlando, he wanted to thank the beautiful girl who had given him the necklace, but for some reason he was completely tongue-tied. As soon as she had gone, he asked Touchstone who she was.

"That, my boy, is Rosalind, Duke Frederick's niece," Touchstone said. "But it's my guess she won't be here for much longer. I've heard the duke's growing tired of having her around – she reminds him too much of her father, the old duke. And now she's gone behind his back and given you that trinket, she'll be in even more trouble."

$$\backsim$$

Over the next few days, Celia noticed that Rosalind no longer thought about her father all the time. She now seemed to spend plenty of time thinking about Orlando instead. As they sat in Celia's room doing their sewing, poor Rosalind could barely concentrate.

"Don't you think he was handsome?" she sighed. "I wonder when I'll see him again. He had such a sweet smile, when he accepted the necklace from me..."

"Rosalind!" Duke Frederick had appeared at the door. Rosalind shook herself out of her daydream.

"I'm afraid your stay here has come to an end," Frederick announced. "I want you to leave."

"But father, why?" pleaded Celia. "What has Rosalind done wrong?"

"No questions," Frederick snapped. "Rosalind, I want you gone by tomorrow."

When he had left the room, Celia hugged her cousin. "Don't worry," she said. I won't be separated from you. If you're leaving, I'm coming with you."

"But – where will we go?" asked Rosalind.

"To the forest, of course, to find your father!"

"What, two young court ladies, wandering through the Forest of Arden by themselves?" laughed Rosalind. "We'll be robbed and murdered in two seconds!"

"Well then, we'll go in disguise," said Celia.

"I've got an idea..." said Rosalind, beginning to smile, "since I'm taller, I'll dress as a boy, and we can pretend to be a brother and sister. I'll call myself Ganymede."

"And I'll call myself Aliena!" said Celia.

"And what if we asked Touchstone to come with us?" Rosalind said. "He'd protect us from strangers! And I will take all my savings, as I can't leave them here."

"It's perfect!" grinned Celia. "Let's go and get ready!"

Although he had been violently forced from his palace and robbed of his power, Duke

Senior had soon grown used to life in the Forest of Arden, and by now he quite liked it.

"You know," he said to his friends and followers, as they sat beneath an oak tree in the spring sunshine, "I may have to go without fine clothes and banquets, and of course I miss my dear daughter Rosalind. But there are so many things about being a duke that I don't miss at all! What a relief it is not to have to worry about politics and listen to false flattery all day long. At least I know that those of you who have followed me here are my true friends – and that's worth more to me than any dukedom!"

Lord Amiens agreed. "It's so relaxing here," he sighed. "The trees, and the river, and the birds singing – I wouldn't change a thing."

"Now, let's go hunting and catch ourselves a deer for supper," said the duke.

Everyone agreed, except Lord Jacques, who was well known for his miserable, melancholy view of life. "It's such a shame for the deer," he complained. "This is their home, and we march in and start shooting them. By taking over this forest, we're just as bad as your brother, who took over your dukedom."

"Don't be silly, Jacques," said Duke Senior. "We've got to eat." And off they went.

The next day, at the palace, Duke Frederick discovered that Celia was missing. He was furious.

"I heard Miss Celia and Miss Rosalind talking about Orlando de Boys," a maidservant told him. "Perhaps they're with him."

"That young whippersnapper who won at the wrestling!" fumed Frederick. "He's sure to have something to do with this! Send for Sir Rowland's oldest son, Oliver. I'll get the truth out of him!"

At that moment, Orlando was about to go to his brother, and ask him for the money he had been promised. But Adam, the old servant, stopped him.

"Don't go in there, sir," he warned. "Oliver has heard how you defeated Charles, and he's in a rage. He won't give you your money – quite the opposite. He's so angry, I'm afraid your life's in danger. You must escape."

"With no money?" Orlando asked. "Where will I go? What will I live on?"

"Sir, you must go to the Forest of Arden," said Adam, "and see if you can find old Duke Senior, who was a friend of your father's." So, without further ado, Orlando set off for the forest.

Rosalind and Celia, disguised as a peasant brother and sister, Ganymede and Aliena, were already in the forest, along with the jester Touchstone. They had been walking all day, and they were exhausted. As they sat down on a log to rest, they heard voices, and saw two shepherds – one an old man, the other much younger.

"Oh, Corin," the boy groaned. "I love her so much, you can't imagine what it's like."

"Of course I can," laughed the old man. "I was in love myself, when I was young."

"No – you could *never* have loved anyone the way I love Phoebe!" the young shepherd declared, then ran off in a sulk.

"Silvius!" the old man called, then gave up, shaking his head.

"Erm – excuse me," Rosalind began, tapping the old shepherd on the shoulder, and making him jump.

"Who are you?" he shouted, waving his crook.

"We are friends," said Rosalind, in her deepest voice. "We mean you no harm. We have come here from the city, and don't know our way – and we need a place to shelter."

"Well then, young sir," said Corin, "maybe I can help you. I know of a cottage near here that's for sale."

"That sounds perfect!" whispered Celia to Rosalind. "Let's buy the cottage, and stay there until we can find out where your father is." And so they followed Corin as he led the way through the trees.

Not far away, Orlando had also arrived in the Forest of Arden. By chance, it was not long before he stumbled across a group of men sitting around a fire, roasting a deer.

"Excuse me," Orlando called. "I'm so tired and hungry. May I join your feast?"

One of the men stood up. "To whom do I have the pleasure of speaking?" he asked. Orlando was surprised to encounter such good manners in such simple surroundings, but he replied politely: "My name is Orlando, son of Sir Rowland de Boys."

"Then you are very welcome, sir. I am Duke Senior, and I knew your father well. You must join us at once, and when you have eaten, tell us how you came here."

❧

"What do you mean, you don't know where he is?" screamed Duke Frederick, shaking Oliver by the throat. "I need to speak to him! My daughter is missing!"

"I – I'm sorry, I can't help you," Oliver spluttered. "Orlando has run away."

"Well, you'd better find him," Frederick snarled. "I'll give you a week. If you don't bring him back to me before seven days are up, I'll seize your house and all your possessions, and throw you out into the street!" And he stormed off.

"I suppose I have no choice," Oliver said to himself. "I'd better go to the forest and look for that brother of mine."

Orlando, meanwhile, had settled into his new life at Duke Senior's forest hideaway. When he wasn't cleaning the camp or helping with the hunting, he spent his time writing love poems to Rosalind, since he still thought about her all the time. He had no idea that she too was in the Forest of Arden, disguised as Ganymede. Nonetheless, he decided to nail his love poems to as many trees as he could, so that everyone for miles around would know how much he loved her.

Unbeknown to Orlando, he was not far away from Rosalind and Celia's cottage. At that moment, Touchstone was sitting outside it talking to Corin, the old shepherd.

"So, sir, how d'you like it living in the countryside?" Corin asked.

"It's alright, I suppose," said Touchstone, "although it's very different from life at court."

"Of course it is!" laughed Corin. "Different customs for different places – that's the way of the world."

*Wherever you find this paper pinned,
I speak my love for Rosalind.
Her name is carried on the wind,
Gorgeous, fair-faced Rosalind.
Tall and pretty, sweet and kind,
The one and only Rosalind.
There's only one thing in my mind
And that's the thought of Rosalind!*

"That's all very well," sighed Touchstone, "but I'm a jester by trade, and there's little chance of being foolish in the forest."

"I wouldn't be so sure about that!" It was Rosalind, coming back from a walk. "Look at this!"

"Ah, it's young Ganymede!" said Corin. "What's that in his hand?"

"It's a poem," said Rosalind. "A love poem! I found it on a tree." She read it aloud.

"Well, that tree yields bad fruit," said Touchstone. "That poem is truly dreadful."

"It doesn't even rhyme properly," Corin complained.

"And look!" It was Celia, following behind Rosalind. "I've found another."

"Stop, stop!" shouted Touchstone, covering his ears. "That's enough bad poetry!"

"Alright, we'll stop," said Celia, "but you and Corin must leave us alone for a while. I need to speak to Ganymede in private."

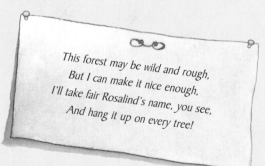

*This forest may be wild and rough,
But I can make it nice enough,
I'll take fair Rosalind's name, you see,
And hang it up on every tree!*

When they had gone, Rosalind asked: "Celia – do you think these poems could be about me?"

"Yes I do!" giggled Celia, bursting with excitement. "And guess who wrote them? It's that boy you like – Orlando! I saw him passing by just now, pinning them to all the trees!"

"Orlando!" Rosalind gasped. "What's he doing here? Oh no! I can't let him see me like this!" But just then, Orlando passed by the cottage, carrying a pile of poems. "Good afternoon," he called to Rosalind and Celia.

"He doesn't recognize us!" Celia whispered. "Go on – talk to him."

"Good afternoon, sir!" Rosalind began. "I am Ganymede, and this is my dear sister Aliena. We're new to these parts."

"So am I," said Orlando, "but welcome to the forest anyway." He shook Rosalind by the hand.

"So," said Rosalind, looking at the papers in Orlando's hand. "These poems are yours, are they?"

"Ah yes," said Orlando, rolling his eyes dreamily. "They tell of Rosalind, the lady I love."

"I'm not sure she'll be impressed by such bad poems," Celia said rudely.

"I'm sorry you don't like them," said Orlando. "The trouble is, I'm afraid I'm not a very good poet."

"You can say that again," said Rosalind, trying to hide her nerves.

"But, sir, you're in luck. It just so happens that I, Ganymede, am an expert in the art of love, and I know exactly what women like. I can teach you how to woo this lady properly, so that you'll really impress her."

"Can you?" Orlando asked, amazed. "That's wonderful! When can we start?"

"This is our cottage," said Rosalind. "Come back and meet me here tomorrow, and I'll give you your first lesson."

When Orlando had gone, Rosalind and Celia both burst out laughing.

"What on earth did you tell him that for?" Celia gasped.

"I don't know – I just had to see him again..." said Rosalind, blushing.

The next day, Rosalind waited at the cottage for Orlando to turn up for his lesson in love. She waited all morning. She waited all afternoon. But he did not appear.

"Oh, where is he?" she moaned to Celia.

Eventually, Corin the shepherd came along, and asked what they were doing. Celia explained that Ganymede was an expert in the art of love, and they were waiting for a friend who was coming to learn more about it.

"Well, if you know so much about love," said Corin, "why don't you come and help young Silvius, who's trying to woo that girl he likes so much, Phoebe. He's making a proper mess of it, and that's for sure."

So, giving up on Orlando, Rosalind and Celia followed Corin. They found Silvius nearby, kneeling on the ground, pleading with a young shepherdess.

"Please, Phoebe, marry me, be mine!" he whined. "I love you so, my heart's set to burst!"

But Phoebe was not interested. "Go away, Silvius!" she snapped.

"Go on, Ganymede – young Silvius needs your help," said Corin, pushing Rosalind forward.

"Erm... excuse me," Rosalind interrupted them. "Young lady," she said, "I can't help but notice that you're not all that pretty, are you? If I were you, I'd accept this boy while you have the chance."

Phoebe spun around and stared at her, and Rosalind realized she probably hadn't helped at all. But as soon as she saw the good-looking young stranger, Phoebe smiled flirtatiously, batting her eyelashes.

"Oh no," said Rosalind. "Don't you go falling in love with me. That will never work!" She turned to Silvius. "And my advice to you, my lad, is to stop being so nice to her. She obviously responds better to rudeness."

"I'd rather hear you being rude to me, than him," Phoebe simpered, sidling up to Rosalind. "Why, I've never seen such a handsome man as you in this forest!"

"Listen, Phoebe," said Rosalind. "You haven't a chance with me, and that's a fact. But now you know how poor Silvius feels, don't you? Can't you have pity on him now? I'm sure he'd make a fine husband for you."

"For goodness' sake!" said Celia. "This is ridiculous. Where's Touchstone when we need him? He could tease this silly girl to her senses!"

"Ah, your jester, you mean?" said Corin. "He's met a shepherdess he likes, too, and gone a wooing. Her name's Audrey."

"It seems everyone's fallen in love, except me," Celia remarked.

"Here I am!" a man's voice called. "Sorry I'm late!" Orlando had arrived for his lesson at last.

❦

Back at the cottage, Rosalind sat Orlando down for his lesson. Just being near him made her tremble and blush, but she pulled her hat down over her face and spoke in her deepest voice. He didn't suspect a thing.

"Now then," she said. "Being late is a very bad start, but we'll do what we can. I'll pretend to be the lady you like – what was her name again?"

"Rosalind," Orlando said.

"Rosalind, that's it – and you can pretend to woo me. How will you start?"

"Well," said Orlando, "if you were really her, I would start by kissing you."

Rosalind blushed even more, but managed to say: "That would be far too hasty!"

"Well then, I would say: 'Rosalind my dearest, I'll die if you don't love me!'"

"Oh, what nonsense!" said Rosalind. "Nobody ever really dies of love, do they?"

"I suppose not," Orlando agreed. "Alright then, I'd say: 'Rosalind, my sweet – will you marry me?'"

"Really? Would you say that?" Rosalind gasped.

"Your voice has gone all squeaky, Ganymede," said Orlando. "Are you alright?"

"Yes, yes of course," Rosalind resumed her deep voice. "Well, if you really are prepared to marry her, we must put you to the test. Aliena!" she called, and Celia came hurrying in from the garden.

"We must have a mock wedding, so that Orlando can see what getting married is like," Rosalind said. "I shall pretend to be Rosalind, his blushing bride. You must play the priest." So Celia, trying to stifle her giggles, pretended to be a priest, and held a mock marriage ceremony.

"Well, this is how it will feel to get married to this Rosalind of yours," Rosalind told Orlando. "Are you sure it's really what you want?"

"Oh, more sure than ever!" said Orlando. Then he looked outside and saw that the sun was going down. "Ganymede – thank you so much for your help," he said, "but I must leave, or my friends will start to wonder where I am. I'll come back tomorrow for another lesson. Goodbye!"

The next day, Rosalind again waited all day, but Orlando did not arrive.

"He's late again!" said Celia. "I know you love him, cousin, but I must say, he doesn't seem very reliable."

"Shhh!" said Rosalind. "Someone's coming – it must be him."

But the man who emerged from the forest, although he looked a little like Orlando, was not him at all. He was older, slightly shorter, and very out of breath.

"Well, I don't know who this is, but he's very good-looking," said Celia, smiling at the stranger.

"Are you Ganymede and Aliena?" the man panted.

"Indeed we are," said Rosalind. "And you are?"

"My name is Oliver de Boys," said the man. "I'm Orlando's brother."

"I didn't know he had a brother!" exclaimed Celia.

"No – well – we haven't been the best of friends," said Oliver. "In fact, until recently, we were the worst of enemies, and when Orlando was in trouble with Duke Frederick, the duke sent me to find him. Well, I came to the forest to look for him, but after a day's searching, I fell asleep under a tree. When I woke up, there was a lion about to pounce on me! I thought I was done for, but just in time, Orlando came along. He fought off the lion, and saved my life."

"Oh! How brave of him!" said Rosalind.

"So, of course, I was very sorry for the way I'd behaved, and asked him if we could be friends again," said Oliver. "And Orlando has forgiven me for the cruelty I've shown him in the past. Now we're both staying in the forest with Duke Senior, until –"

"Duke Senior!?" gasped Rosalind. Did this mean her father was living close by?

"Yes," said Oliver, "his camp's not far away from here. Orlando is resting there now, recovering from the wounds the lion gave him – and so he's sent me here to apologize to you. He said he had a meeting with you, and he's sorry he missed it."

It was all too much for Rosalind. Forgetting her disguise, she cried: "Oh! he's such a perfect gentleman!" and fainted.

But Oliver and Celia hardly noticed. They were too busy gazing into each others' eyes.

The next morning, Orlando
and Oliver made their way to the
little cottage in the forest together.

"Are you really sure you're in love
with Ganymede's sister?" Orlando asked.

"I'm just as sure as you are about this Rosalind you
keep talking about!" said Oliver. "And this morning I'm going to ask
Aliena if she'll marry me."

"Well, if you're that sure, you have my blessing, brother," said
Orlando, and the brothers hugged each other.

When they arrived at the cottage, they saw Rosalind and Celia sitting
outside. "Ganymede!" Orlando called. "It's good to see you! I'm sorry about yesterday!"

"Aliena!" Oliver shouted. "I've come to ask if you'll marry me!"

"Yes! Yes, I will!" Celia squealed, and ran into his arms.

"Isn't this good news?" Rosalind said to Orlando, as they watched the happy
couple talking together.

"Well, I'm delighted for them both, but I'm jealous as well," Orlando replied. "I wish my beloved Rosalind were here, and then I could ask her to marry me too. Then my brother and I could celebrate our new-found friendship with a joint wedding."

"Well, Orlando," said Rosalind, as a brilliant idea came into her head. "Besides my knowledge of love, I am also able to see into the future. And I can tell you that if you come to my cottage again tomorrow, you will find Rosalind here."

"Really? That's amazing!" said Orlando. "I'll make sure I'm here."

Just then, Silvius and Phoebe appeared. Silvius was still pleading with Phoebe to marry him. Phoebe was still looking annoyed. She came up to Rosalind, and said: "Silvius still says he loves me, but Ganymede, it's you I really like. Do you love me, Ganymede?"

"I'm afraid there is no woman I love," said Rosalind, truthfully.

"What, you've never been in love at all?" demanded Phoebe. "Silvius, tell Ganymede what being in love feels like, and then maybe he'll have pity on me."

"Why," said Silvius, "being in love is like... it's like being all made of sighs and tears, with a head full of fantasy and make-believe. You adore your beloved, and feel cross with them too. You'd wait for them forever, and yet you feel impatient. Your heart's in a mess, and your head's in a muddle. And that's how I feel about Phoebe!"

"And that's exactly how I feel about you, Ganymede!" said Phoebe.

"And that's just how I feel about Rosalind!" cried Orlando.

"Well, as I said," Rosalind declared, "I don't feel like that about any woman."

"I do!" It was Touchstone. He came skipping up to the cottage, leading a pretty young shepherd girl by the hand. "This is Audrey," he grinned. "She's agreed to marry me! Isn't she lovely? I never knew the countryside could be so much fun!" he cried, dancing his girlfriend around and around.

"Right," said Rosalind. "I have just one question to ask. Phoebe, if you knew, without a doubt, that you could not marry me, would you agree to marry Silvius?"

"Oh, I suppose so," said Phoebe.

"Good. In that case, everyone listen to me. I want you all to come back here tomorrow morning, wearing your best clothes. Bring your friends and families, and Orlando, you must bring Duke Senior and his men. Does everyone understand?"

Everyone did. As soon as they had left, Rosalind went to find the nearest church.

Everyone did. As soon as they had left, Rosalind went to find the nearest church.

144

The next morning, a huge crowd of people gathered outside the cottage. Among them were Oliver, Orlando and Duke Senior.

"And this young man, Ganymede, said that Rosalind would be here?" the duke asked Orlando.

"He did," said Orlando. "I'm sure you'll see your daughter again soon!"

"Well, if I do, you have my consent to ask her to marry you," the duke smiled.

At that moment, Rosalind, still disguised as Ganymede, came out of the cottage.

"So," she called, "Oliver, you say you'll marry Aliena?"

"I will," said Oliver.

"And Touchstone, you'll marry Audrey?" Touchstone stepped forward and bowed.

"And Phoebe, you'll marry Silvius – if you can't marry me?" Phoebe nodded.

"And if Rosalind were here, Orlando, you'd marry her?"

"Of course!"

"Then let's go to the church!" Rosalind cried, pulling off her hat, and letting her long dark hair fall down. "There'll be four weddings today!"

"My daughter!" wailed the duke, with tears in his eyes.

"My beloved!" shouted Orlando. They both ran and threw their arms around her.

"And this, by the way, is not Aliena," Rosalind announced. "It's Celia!"

They were all about to set off for the church, when, a young man squeezed through the crowd. "Oliver! Orlando!" he called. It was Jake, their middle brother.

"I came back from school and you weren't there!" he shouted. "I have news from the court... Duke Frederick has relented! He's decided to let Duke Senior have his dukedom back!"

The people cheered even more loudly, and lifted Duke Senior onto their shoulders as they made their way to the church. There, the four couples were married. Then Touchstone serenaded the crowd with his singing, and everyone danced until they could dance no more.

*It was a lover and his lass,*
*With a hey, and a ho, and a hey nonino,*
*That o'er the green corn-field did pass,*
*In the spring time, the only pretty ring time,*
*When birds do sing, hey ding a ding, ding;*
*Sweet lovers love the spring.*

# The Winter's Tale

For almost a year, King Polixenes of Bohemia had been staying with his friend, King Leontes of Sicily, and Queen Hermione, his beautiful wife. The two kings had been friends since they were boys, and Polixenes had enjoyed his visit very much. But now it was nearly winter, and it was time for him to go home.

"I'm so sorry to leave," Polixenes told his hosts. "But I should be at home ruling my people, and I miss my little son. You've been so kind, I don't know how to thank you."

"By staying longer!" said Hermione. "We'll miss you so much when you're gone."

"It's very tempting, but – I must go," said Polixenes. "I'll set sail tomorrow."

"So soon!" said Leontes. "Couldn't you stay just one more day?"

"Oh, please do," Hermione begged him, squeezing his hand.

Polixenes smiled. "Well, perhaps just a day," he said.

Leontes smiled too, but inside, his heart ached to see his wife and Polixenes holding hands. He was sure they felt more than just friendship for each other. In fact, Leontes suspected that his friend was in love with the queen, and she with him.

Just then, five-year-old Prince Mamillius ran into the room. "Come and play with me, daddy," he called.

"Isn't he a fine young man!" said Polixenes. "He reminds me so much of my Florizel."

Leontes picked his son up. "I'm going to play with Mamillius," he said. "Hermione, you entertain our guest in the meantime."

"Of course!" his wife said, playfully pulling Polixenes to his feet. "We'll go walking in the garden."

*Walking in the garden!* Leontes thought to himself in a panic. Surely that was the kind of activity they would only engage in if they were in love! But he tried to calm himself down while he helped Mamillius with his building blocks and toy animals.

Later, though, Leontes sent for his most trusted advisor, Camillo. He had to tell someone how worried he was about his wife's feelings for his friend.

"Sir, you insult your wife to think such a thing," said Camillo, when he heard about the king's fears. "I assure you, it's nothing."

"Is holding hands nothing?" Leontes demanded. "And whispering, and giggling, and walking in the garden arm in arm? Is that nothing?"

"They're just being friendly," Camillo said. "You should be glad your wife and your best friend get along so well. And Hermione would never betray you. Can't you see that?"

But Leontes couldn't. In his mind, the evidence was plain to see. Almost in tears, he grabbed Camillo's arm, and whispered: "Camillo, I know they're in love, I just *know* it! Polixenes was my best friend, but now he's my enemy! I need you to do something for me. You must fetch some rat poison from the kitchens, and put it in his wine. It will be easy."

Camillo was shocked. "What, kill him?" he gasped. "Your majesty, this is ridiculous!"

"So," Leontes accused him, "you're helping them, are you? Keeping secrets for them?"

"I'm not, sir!" said Camillo. He was horrified to see how deluded the king was.

"Then if you really are my loyal servant, you'll do this for me."

Although he knew that he could not possibly do such a terrible thing, Camillo had no choice but to pretend he would. "Very well, sir," he said. "I'll do it."

Soon after Leontes had left the room, Polixenes came in.

"Camillo," he said. "I wanted to talk to you in private. I'm a little worried about Leontes – he seems angry with me, but I don't know why."

"Oh, sir," sighed Camillo. "I fear the king is not well."

"What's wrong with him?" said Polixenes.

"A disease of the mind, sir – a delusion. He thinks you and Hermione are – well, he thinks you're in love, and plotting against him."

"What?" gasped Polixenes. "I would never do that to him! And nor would she!"

"I know, sir, but I can't persuade him," said Camillo. "The truth is, he's so convinced, he's asked me to murder you! You must escape as soon as you can."

"Murder me?" said Polixenes, turning pale.

"Sir, I am a senior advisor, and the servants will do my bidding. I can arrange for you to leave tonight under cover of darkness – it's the safest thing to do until Leontes sees sense. And, if you will let me, I'll come too, for when the king finds out I've helped you I won't be able to stay here. Maybe I could come back with you and serve you in Bohemia?"

"Camillo, of course you can. It's the least I can do. You've saved my life."

The next day, Queen Hermione and her lady-in-waiting, Emilia, were playing with Mamillius.

"You're mother's going to have another baby soon," Emilia told Mamillius.

"That's right," said Hermione. "The baby's inside my tummy. Soon it will be born, and then you'll have a little brother or sister to play with."

While they were talking, Leontes came in with a group of advisors and servants.

"It's true, your majesty," Lord Cleomenes was saying. "Polixenes is gone, and Camillo too. According to the guards, they left in the middle of the night."

"So I was right!" Leontes fumed. "Camillo *was* helping them! He's been on their side all along! Well," he said furiously, striding over to Hermione, "the two of them might be gone, but you're still here – and I'm going to make you pay for this!"

"Leontes?" said Hermione. "What are you talking about?"

"You know very well what I'm talking about!" Leontes shouted. "You and Polixenes! How long has it been going on?"

"Me and Polixenes? What do you mean?" said Hermione. "Please Leontes, you're talking nonsense – don't say this. You'll be so sorry when you realize you're wrong."

"I've heard enough lies!" Leontes screamed. "Guards! Take her to the dungeons!"

"Sir, you can't do that!" Emilia said. "She's pregnant!" But Leontes ignored her.

"At least let me take Emilia with me!" Hermione cried as she was dragged away. Leaving Mamillius with one of the maidservants, Emilia hurried after her.

"Are you sure about this, your majesty?" said another of the king's advisors, Lord Antigonus. "The QUEEN seems innocent to me."

"Indeed – there is no evidence of any wrongdoing," said Lord Cleomenes gently.

"No evidence!?" Leontes roared. "What about Camillo running off with Polixenes? He was helping them, and now he's disappeared – that's all the proof I need."

However hard they tried, the lords couldn't change the king's mind. But they did persuade him to send two messengers to visit the Oracle – a sacred shrine, where there lived a priestess who could answer people's questions and predict the future. The messengers were told to ask the priestess whether Hermione had really been unfaithful to Leontes. Until they returned, Leontes said, she must stay in the dungeons.

Paulina clutched her candle tightly as she stepped down the dark, slippery stone stairway that led to the dungeons. She was the wife of Lord Antigonus, and a close friend of Hermione's. When she heard what had happened, she went to visit Hermione at once.

But when the jailer saw her, he shook his head. "She's not allowed visitors," he said.

"Then please bring Emilia here," said Paulina, "and I'll give her a message to take back to the QUEEN."

The jailer grunted and went to fetch Emilia.

"Oh, my lady," Emilia cried, as soon as she saw Paulina waiting for her. "Hermione's just had her baby in the dungeon – a little girl! It's not right for them to be in prison."

"Poor Hermione!" said Paulina. "Surely the king should know about this?"

"It would be best if you and Antigonus told him," said Emilia.

"I have an idea," said Paulina. "Why don't I take the baby with me? When Leontes sees his new little daughter, she's sure to melt his hard heart."

Emilia went to ask Hermione, and they all agreed on the plan. So, with the little girl in her arms, Pauline carefully climbed the stone steps and went to find Leontes.

The king was pacing up and down in his study. He was still tortured by the thought of his wife and his best friend both betraying him. Not to mention Camillo, whom he had thought he could trust. They had all turned against him!

A servant knocked on the door and peered around it. "Your majesty," he said. "Little Mamillius is unwell, sir. Since his mother was thrown in the dungeons, he's had a terrible fever."

"I'll think about that later," Leontes snapped, and the servant left. A moment later, there was another knock at the door.

"What now!?" Leontes yelled.

"It's me and Paulina," Lord Antigonus called. "There's someone we'd like you to meet." They came in, Paulina holding the baby out in front of her.

"Take it away," Leontes said angrily.

"This is your new baby girl," said Paulina.

"Can't you control your wife, Antigonus?" Leontes shouted. "Tell her to take the child away."

"At least I trust my wife," Antigonus said, "and I know she's only trying to do what's best for you. Come on, don't you even want to hold your beautiful daughter?"

"Didn't you hear me – I said *take it away*!" Leontes screamed. "I have no desire to see the child of that cheating wife of mine!"

"How dare you say that about the queen?" said Paulina angrily, "when you have no evidence – nothing but your own silly imaginings! How can you do this to her? Look," she went on, carefully laying the baby down in front of him. "Look – she looks just like you."

"Will you send your stupid wife away!" Leontes yelled at Antigonus, and Paulina finally left the room in tears.

Then Leontes said: "So you set Paulina up to this, did you, Antigonus?"

"I didn't, sir, I swear. Paulina cares for you and the queen. She's trying to help you."

"Well, she doesn't know what's best for me; I do. And I order you to take that baby away and throw it in the fire. That will teach Hermione a lesson."

"Sir, I won't do that," Antigonus said. "Hermione and the baby are both innocent."

"Very well," said Leontes. "Then take the child away, to another country. I don't care where. You can leave it out on a hillside to take its chances. Do it now!"

"I'll take her," said Antigonus, his voice trembling with anger. "Indeed sir, she'll be safer with the wild animals than she is here with you." And he took the baby and left the room.

When he had gone, yet another servant arrived. "The messengers are back from the Oracle, sir," he said, "with a letter from the priestess."

"Good," said Leontes. "We'll hold a court hearing tomorrow and put Hermione on trial. Bring her to the great hall tomorrow morning."

The next day, Hermione found herself in chains in the great hall of the palace, a guard on either side of her. All the lords and ladies and servants sat waiting for the trial to begin. Leontes sat at the far end of the hall, on his throne, wearing his crown.

"Let us begin," he announced. "Read the charges."

A servant stepped forward, opened a scroll, and read: "Hermione, Queen of Sicily, is accused of treason. She has betrayed the king by giving her love to Polixenes, King of Bohemia, and she has plotted with him against her husband."

"Well?" Leontes asked her, coldly.

Hermione looked him in the eye. "Since I have no way of proving it," she said quietly, "it won't help me much to say I am not guilty. But I will say it anyway, for it is true. I am not guilty. And if the gods are watching – as I believe they are – *they* will know I speak the truth. Leontes, I have been your wife for eight happy years, and I have never betrayed you. Why would I change now?"

"And what about Camillo?" Leontes sneered.

"I don't know why Camillo ran away," said Hermione, "but I know he's an honest man."

"You're hiding things from me!" Leontes shouted, pointing at her, "and you'll pay for it! The punishment for treason is death!"

"You can threaten me all you like," said Hermione. "I'm not afraid of death. My life is worthless now – shut up in prison, away from my children and my friends. But I do care for my reputation, and I have been wrongly accused. Why don't we consult the Oracle?"

"Very well," said Leontes. "Where are the messengers?"

The two men stepped forward. "You have the letter from the priestess?" Leontes asked, and they nodded. "Then let's hear it," Leontes said.

One of the men broke the seal and opened the letter.

"Sir, it says: 'Hermione is innocent. Polixenes is innocent. Camillo is an honest man. And Leontes shall have no heir to his throne, if that which is lost is not found again.'"

A sigh of relief spread around the hall. Surely Leontes would set Hermione free now!

But Leontes looked furious. "The Oracle is nonsense!" he shouted, and all the lords and ladies stared at him in horror. "The trial will continue."

Before the trial could go any further, however, a servant came rushing in. "Your majesty!" he cried. "Oh sir, it's Prince Mamillius. He's – he's died, sir, of his illness."

Hermione gasped, and fainted onto the floor. Paulina and Emilia rushed to her side.

"Stop the trial," said Leontes weakly. "Take Hermione away..." he called. As the lords and ladies and servants left the hall, Leontes sank back down onto his throne, his head in his hands.

"Oh, what have I done!?" he groaned to himself. He thought of the words of the Oracle, which said that he would have no heir. Mamillius was his heir, and now he was dead. And if that was true, the rest of the Oracle was true too. Hermione was innocent. And Leontes was sure he was being punished by the gods for his foolishness and cruelty.

He resolved to put things right as soon as he could. He would go to Hermione and beg her forgiveness. He would write to Polixenes and Camillo with his deepest apologies. And he must stop Antigonus from leaving with the baby...

"Sir?" It was Paulina. Leontes looked up.

"Your majesty... I'm very sorry, but Hermione is dead. It was the shock of losing both her children, sir – she could not bear it..."

"No... oh no... I have destroyed everything..." Leontes whispered, clutching at his face. "Oh Paulina – I have been so stupid. All I have left is my baby – my little daughter."

"Antigonus has already taken the baby away," said Paulina quietly. "We'll have to wait until he returns."

But Antigonus was never to return. Before he left,
he and Paulina had taken the baby to Hermione one last
time so that she could say goodbye. Antigonus had
promised to leave the child somewhere safe, where she would
soon be found and rescued. Hermione had named her Perdita, which means "lost," and
they wrote a note asking whoever found her to raise her as their own. They filled a box
with gold pieces to pay for Perdita's upbringing, and Hermione put the necklace she was
wearing into the box too.

Then, following the king's orders, Antigonus took the child across the sea to
Bohemia, the land of King Polixenes. The sailors took him to a remote shore, and
Antigonus carried the baby, along with the letter and the box of gold, a little way inland.

He walked until he saw sheep and barns and cottages, and knew that shepherds
and farmers must be nearby. Then he gently put Perdita down on a soft tussock of grass,
wrapped her blanket around her, pinned the letter to it, and put the box of gold pieces
beside her. A storm was brewing, and he hoped someone would find her soon.

"Goodbye, sweet child," Antigonus said. "May the gods watch over you. Have a
happy life, my little one." Then he kissed her and stood up to make his way back to the ship.

But, as he turned around, he saw a huge bear lumbering towards him. Terrified it
might find the baby, he shouted and threw stones to distract it, and it began to chase him.
Some distance away, it caught him, and that was the end of Lord Antigonus.

❧

Not long afterwards, an old shepherd came along to round up his sheep, and heard a baby
crying. He followed the noise, and found Perdita lying on the ground.

"What a pretty little thing!" the shepherd gasped. "What can this be about?"

Just then a younger shepherd came along. "You'll never guess what I've seen!" he
said. "There was a fine ship, moored just off the shore, and it was all wrecked by the
storm, tossed to and fro until it sank like a toy – and all the sailors are drowned. And
what's more, just down by the river, a bear has killed someone! It's not anyone from
around here – he was wearing expensive clothes, like a lord or a prince. The bear's still
eating him now!"

"Bless their poor souls!" said the old man. "And look what I've found — a little baby!" He bent down and took up the letter. "I can't read," he said. "You tell me what it says."

The young man read the letter. "Well, it says she is called Perdita," he said, "and begs for her to be cared for — the gold in the box will pay for it. Gold in the box!" he gasped, and they opened the box to find it packed with gold coins, with the necklace lying on top. "And it says the little girl is always to wear the necklace," the young man read. "Why, sir, you'll be rich if you take this baby on!"

"Richer than gold," said the old shepherd, "for my wife and I never had any children, and we've always longed for a daughter. I will take her home, and my wife will love her and care for her as if she were her own little baby. As for the gold, we'll use some of it to pay for a funeral for that poor gentleman, and those unfortunate sailors."

Back in Sicily, King Leontes lived in suffering and sorrow. He never remarried, but spent his days weeping for his lost children and his poor beloved wife, and regretting the terrible mistake that had cost him his family and his dear friends Polixenes and Camillo.

He was so ashamed that he shut himself away in his palace, and grew thin and pale. He saw no one but his servants and his loyal friend Paulina. When Antigonus had not returned, she too had suffered terribly, and she sympathized with the king. She passed on his orders, so that Sicily was still ruled properly, and she listened to his pain and comforted him. And in this way, sixteen years went by.

Leontes often wrote to Polixenes and Camillo. But when Polixenes had heard about Hermione's death, he refused to forgive his old friend, and would not write back.

But Camillo missed Leontes, and he missed Sicily too. After many years had passed, he decided he would like to see his old homeland again, and should perhaps visit Leontes. So he went to Polixenes and told him he would like go to Sicily.

"But Camillo," said Polixenes. "You're my best servant – I don't want to lose you."

"It will just be a short visit," said Camillo. "But I must see my homeland."

"Very well then," said Polixenes. "But please, don't leave just yet. I have a problem I need you to help me with. My son Florizel is disobeying me. He should be at his lessons, and attending to his princely duties, but he's always sneaking off to the countryside in western Bohemia. I haven't even seen him for the last three days!"

"Now you mention it, nor have I," said Camillo. "What can he be up to?"

"They say he stays at the house of a shepherd," Polixenes said.

"Aha," said Camillo. "I've heard tell of an old shepherd in those parts who has the most beautiful daughter ever seen."

"Exactly," said Polixenes miserably. "I'm afraid that's the very reason Florizel keeps going there. But I can't have him falling in love with a shepherd girl – that would never do! Let's disguise ourselves, and go and visit the shepherd to see what's going on."

"An excellent plan," said Camillo.

Polixenes was right about Florizel, for the young prince had fallen in love with the shepherd's daughter, who was none other than Perdita. Now sixteen years old, she had indeed become the most beautiful girl in Bohemia. No one knew it, but with her fair hair, deep brown eyes and radiant smile, she looked very like her mother, Queen Hermione.

When Prince Florizel had first seen her, on an official visit to a country fair, he'd longed to know who she was. He had followed her to her father's house, disguising himself as a shepherd boy named Doricles. Perdita liked him just as much as he liked her, and the two of them had soon become inseparable. The locals gossiped about who the young man was and where he had come from, but only Perdita knew the truth.

When Polixenes and Camillo arrived at the old shepherd's cottage, disguised as weary travellers, the old man was alone. He said they were welcome to stay, but since his wife had died, he only had his daughter Perdita to cook and clean for him. She was out at the sheep-shearing, so he asked them to go with him into the fields to find her.

They found Perdita and Florizel in a meadow with all the other young shepherds and shepherdesses. The shearing was done, and they were dancing, singing and laughing.

"Perdita," the old shepherd called. "You must come home now. We have visitors."

When Perdita turned around, Camillo gasped. "Why, she is incredibly beautiful," he said. Even Polixenes had to admit she was the prettiest girl he'd ever seen. Another dance began, and Perdita danced with Florizel.

"Who's that young man?" asked Polixenes, though he knew very well who it was.

"They call him Doricles," said the old shepherd, "and he's in love with my daughter. I dare say they'll get married. He's a fine young man."

Finally, the shepherd persuaded Perdita to come back to the cottage, and Doricles came too. On the way, Polixenes whispered to Camillo: "It's even worse that I thought! I cannot allow them to get married!"

"But she's so lovely," Camillo said, "and they're so happy together."

"She's a shepherdess!" hissed Polixenes. "I will *not* let him marry her!"

Back at the cottage, Polixenes started to ask "Doricles" some awkward questions.

"So, Doricles," he said, "if you love this girl, why haven't you bought her any gifts?"

"I'm just a shepherd," he replied. "I can't afford gifts. I only have love to give her."

"And that's all I want," said Perdita. "I'm as happy as can be with him."

"So," asked Polixenes, "you intend to marry her, do you?"

Florizel blushed. "I do," he said, "if she'll have me. For I love her, and whatever riches I had, even if I was the king, it would mean nothing to me if she wasn't there."

"Oh!" cried the shepherd. "Just as I hoped! Perdita, my dear, do you feel the same?"

"Exactly the same!" said Perdita. "I love him and I want to marry him."

"Well, you know you have my permission," the old shepherd said.

"Wait a minute!" Polixenes interrupted. "What about your father, young man? You do have a father, I take it? What does he have to say about this?"

"I'm not telling him about it," Florizel said.

"Why not? I think a father has a right to know about such things," said Polixenes.

"I'm sorry, sir," said Florizel, "but I don't plan to tell my father. He wouldn't like it."

"You're right, I don't like it one bit!" Polixenes shouted, throwing off his disguise, "and I forbid it. Florizel, you can't marry a shepherd girl!"

"Florizel?" the old shepherd stammered. "Prince Florizel? Oh mercy me! And you are King Polixenes! Oh, your majesty, forgive me – I had no idea it was you!"

"Your majesty," said Perdita. "The same sun that shines upon your palace shines on our little cottage. I love your son and he loves me. That should be good enough for anyone."

"Hush, Perdita," the old shepherd said. "Don't speak to the king like that!"

But Polixenes ignored her. "You will not let this marriage go ahead, and that is a royal order," he told the shepherd. "If you do, you'll be thrown in jail." And he walked out.

"I knew this would happen!" Perdita wept. "Oh Florizel, what are we to do?"

"I won't give you up," said Florizel. "I *will* marry you, and we'll run away together."

"Don't do that!" the shepherd wailed. "He'll throw me in jail!"

"Might I make a suggestion?" said Camillo, and they all turned to him.

"I am planning a trip to Sicily to visit my old master, King Leontes," said Camillo. "He was once Polixenes's dear friend, and longs to hear from him. I think you should both come with me. Florizel, you can tell Leontes that Polixenes has sent you, and he'll welcome you with open arms. You can get married there. Then I'll write to Polixenes with the news, and he'll have to accept it. Surely that's better than running away to some unknown place on your own? And as for you, sir," he said to the shepherd, "if you are sent to jail, I will arrange for you to be released."

They all agreed, and Camillo, Florizel and Perdita set off for Sicily at once.

In Sicily, Leontes was sitting in his palace, talking to Paulina, when a servant came in.

"You have visitors, your majesty," he said. Leontes looked up. He never had visitors.

"Prince Florizel of Bohemia is here, sir, with his fiancée," said the servant, "and she's the most beautiful girl I ever saw."

"What – prettier than Hermione was?" said Paulina.

"Indeed so," the messenger replied.

"Maybe Polixenes has finally forgiven me, if he's sent his son to visit me," Leontes said.

"Send them in," said Paulina.

Florizel and Perdita were shown in, and Leontes stared at them in amazement. "Why, Florizel!" he cried, unable to stop himself from rushing over and hugging the boy. "You look just like your father! And you, young lady – you are absolutely beautiful."

Then Leontes felt tears coming to his eyes. "If my children had lived," he said, "they would be about the same ages as you two are now. But I lost them, and the love of your father too, Florizel, though I long with all my heart to be friends with him again."

"Well," said Florizel, "my father has sent me to say he longs to see you too. But he's getting old, and did not want to travel just yet, until he heard how you responded."

Just then another servant came in. "More visitors, sir," he said. "King Polixenes himself is here. He says his son has run off with a shepherd girl, and he wants to know if they're here. He has the young lady's father with him, sir – he's just a humble shepherd."

"So you lied to me," said Leontes, turning to the young couple.

"I'm sorry, sir," said Florizel. "It's true – we were running away from my father, not bringing you his greetings. We want to get married, but he won't let us, so we came here. Camillo helped us."

"Camillo?" said Leontes. "Is he here?"

"He's waiting outside," said Florizel.

"Leontes, take this chance to make amends," said Paulina. "Go and greet your old friends and apologize to them, and sort this situation out." Yet she could barely speak, for she had seen the necklace around the girl's neck, and realized how like Hermione she looked.

"Yes," said Leontes, "I will. And having no children of my own, I will speak for these two and take their side." And taking Paulina, Florizel and Perdita with him, he went to see his guests.

"Polixenes..." Leontes began, when he saw his old friend. "And Camillo... oh, my comrades, can you ever forgive me?"

"Leontes!" Camillo threw his arms around his old master.

"Leontes, my dear old friend," said Polixenes, hugging him tightly. "Why don't we let bygones be bygones. It's so good to see you!"

"Thank you," Leontes wept. "I am so sorry for what I did, and I regret it every day, for my mistake cost me my family. But these two young people have asked me to help them, and so I will. Polixenes, you can see your son is in love, and what a wonderful girl he has found. May he not marry her?"

"She's a shepherdess!" said Polixenes. "Florizel must marry someone more suitable."

"Who cares about that, when you have true love?" said Leontes. "That's what I had with Hermione, and I threw it away. Don't let such a thing happen again, my friend. If they truly love each other – why, then a shepherdess is as good as a princess."

"Actually, she's not my real daughter – that's what I've been trying to tell you," said the old shepherd. "She was a foundling, and it's my guess she came from a wealthy family, since they left gold with her, and a letter, and the necklace that she always wears."

And he told them how he had found Perdita, sixteen years ago, on a tussock of grass in the meadow near his cottage.

"Perdita..." whispered Paulina. "That is what her mother called her. And the gold and the letter and the necklace – those are the things we sent with her!"

"With who?" asked Leontes.

"With your daughter," said Paulina, "your baby daughter!" She began to cry as she explained how Antigonus had left the necklace with the baby, and the letter saying she must always wear it. When Leontes looked closely at the jewel around Perdita's neck, he remembered it from many years before, when he had given it to Hermione on her birthday.

Perdita's eyes filled with tears as she took Leontes by the hand. "Father..." she said.

"My daughter..." Leontes sobbed. "My daughter – my dearest, forgive me for sending you away! And to you, sir," he said to the shepherd, "a thousand thanks for saving her!"

"So Antigonus performed his task well," said Paulina. "But what became of him?"

"You mean the gentleman who left her in the meadow?" the old shepherd asked.

"Yes," said Paulina. "He was my husband."

"Oh Madam, I'm so sorry," said the shepherd. "The gentleman was eaten by a bear, and his ship was wrecked, his sailors all lost. We used the gold to give them a proper burial."

"Oh, my poor Antigonus," Paulina wept, and Camillo put his arms around her.

Finally, Polixenes said, "Let's have no more unhappiness. If these two young people want to be married, I have no objection."

～

And so everyone was forgiven, and Leontes and Polixenes set about arranging a grand royal wedding for their children, with fireworks and feasting for all the citizens of Sicily.

Two days before the wedding was to take place, Paulina found Leontes discussing last-minute details with Polixenes, Camillo, Florizel and Perdita, and the old shepherd.

"Leontes," Paulina said. "There is something I'd like to show you."

Leontes looked up, smiling. "Of course," he said. "What is it?"

"I have had a statue of Hermione made, to remember her by," said Paulina. "I would like to give it to you as a gift." So they all followed her, and Paulina took them to a room with a curtain drawn across it. She pulled it aside, and there stood a beautiful statue of Hermione, painted in full, lifelike detail, and dressed in royal robes.

Leontes stared. "What a likeness!" he said. "How perfectly the sculptor has captured her! But Paulina," he said, "Hermione was twenty-six when she died. This statue is of an older woman."

"Ah, that's the cunning art of the sculptor," said Paulina. "I asked him to make her look just as she would now, if she were still alive."

"She's lovely," said Perdita, gazing at the statue. "Since I cannot ever meet my real mother, I will kiss the statue's hand."

"No!" said Paulina. "The paint is still wet. Don't touch."

"It's amazing," said Leontes. "To see it fills my heart with feelings! Oh, how I still miss her, after all these years!"

"I can make the statue move, too," said Paulina, smiling to herself, "for it's a magic statue, you know."

"Really?" gasped Leontes, "Oh, please show us."

"Very well," said Paulina. "Statue, come to life."

The statue slowly moved, stepped off its plinth and came towards them. Leontes couldn't help himself – he reached out and touched it. "Oh, she's warm!" he cried.

Then the statue opened its mouth and spoke. "My daughter... my husband..." it said, in a voice trembling with tears.

It was the real Hermione.

"I am alive," she said. "Paulina has kept me hidden all these years. I was so upset about losing my children that I sent word I was dead, and refused ever to reveal myself until my daughter was found."

Leontes had never thought he would feel such joy again. He threw his arms around his dear wife and his beloved daughter, who had been restored to him after so long, and resolved never to hurt them again.

# Shakespeare's life and works

# Who was Shakespeare?

## Shakespeare's life

William Shakespeare was an English playwright (writer of plays) who became one of the world's most famous writers. Although he lived around 400 years ago, his plays are still performed all over the world, and he is regarded as one of the greatest writers in history.

Shakespeare was born in 1564 in Stratford, a small town in central England. After marrying a local woman, Anne Hathaway, and having three children, he went to London to make his fortune. He worked as an actor and as a playwright. He also helped to run a theatre company and became joint owner of a theatre in London called the Globe. The original Globe Theatre is no longer standing, but a working replica of it opened in London in 1996.

His life and work in London made Shakespeare a rich man. He was able to buy his family a large, expensive house in Stratford, called New Place, and at the end of his life he retired there. He died in Stratford in 1616, aged about 52.

## Shakespeare's stories

Shakespeare wrote his plays to be performed on the stage, and they were only published as books afterwards. In Shakespeare's day, since there was no radio, TV or movies, people often went to the theatre for something to do. Going to see a play was not regarded as a special occasion, but as an everyday entertainment – similar to watching a TV soap opera today. People wanted to see exciting, funny and scary things on the stage, so playwrights like Shakespeare had to choose interesting subjects for their plays. Shakespeare wrote about things like murder, betrayal, war, love affairs, ghosts, practical jokes, adventures and disguises to keep his audience interested.

In fact, although Shakespeare brought lots of exciting stories to the stage, he rarely made the stories up himself. Instead he borrowed them from earlier writers, such as the English poet Chaucer, the ancient Greek poet Homer, and the Italian storyteller Giovanni Boccaccio. Or he wrote plays about real historical people, such as Julius Caesar, Macbeth or Richard III. He often took two or three popular stories and combined them into one play. The tales in this book are taken from ten of Shakespeare's most popular plays. You can read condensed versions of his other 28 plays on pages 166-189.

# Shakespeare's works

## Plays

Most of Shakespeare's works are plays – he wrote nearly 40 altogether. They are mainly written in a kind of non-rhyming poetry known as blank verse. Shakespeare wrote several types of plays:

**Tragedies** are plays with a tragic ending. They usually have an important main character called the protagonist, who starts off as a good person but, thanks to bad luck, poor decisions and other mistakes, ends up on a downward spiral. For example, in *Macbeth*, Macbeth is the central character. He starts off as a good soldier, but his desire for the crown leads him astray, and he dies an evil criminal. Other tragedies by Shakespeare include *Hamlet*, *King Lear* and *Othello*.

**Comedies** are plays with happy endings. They are usually about couples falling in love and overcoming obstacles on their way to happiness. They often have comic characters such as clowns and rude servants (although Shakespeare's other plays, even the tragedies, can have funny scenes too). Most of the comedies end with celebrations as one or more couples get engaged or married. Famous Shakespeare comedies include *Twelfth Night* and *A Midsummer Night's Dream*.

**Problem plays** are comedies with a dark side. Shakespeare didn't call them problem plays – it's just a modern name for them. They have happy endings, but not all the characters end up happy. Sometimes they deal with difficult issues. For example, *All's Well That Ends Well* ends with a husband being forced to stay with a wife he doesn't really love, and *The Merchant of Venice* deals with racist attitudes and shows how unfair life can be.

**Romances** are another type of comedy that Shakespeare wrote towards the end of his career. They are magical adventure stories in which people go on long journeys. Instead of ending with marriages, these plays are usually about people changing as they grow older, and often end with parents being reunited with their grown-up children. The romances include *The Tempest* and *The Winter's Tale*.

**History plays** are plays about real-life characters from English history. Because they are from real life, they don't always have the most exciting plots, but some have very vivid characters. For example, *Henry V* is about a great king who triumphs in battle against all odds, and *Richard III* is about an evil king who murders anyone who stands in his way. In some of his history plays, Shakespeare changed the historical facts to make the story more interesting, or to avoid offending the real-life relatives of the characters.

## Poetry

Besides plays, Shakespeare wrote poetry. Some of it is rarely read today, but his sonnets (a type of short poem) are still very well known. There's more about Shakespeare's poetry on page 190.

# All's Well That Ends Well

Type of play: Problem play
Written: c.1602
In brief: Helena loves Bertram and wins his hand in marriage, but he runs away. She has to resort to trickery to get him back.

## Main characters

Helena..........................................A clever young lady, the daughter of a doctor
Bertram........................................Young count of Rousillon in France, and servant of the French king
Countess of Rousillon...................Helena's kindly old guardian, and ruler of Rousillon in France
King of France............................ Friend of the countess, and Bertram's employer
Parolles........................................Bertrams' lazy, boastful, good-for-nothing best friend
Diana.......................................... A young woman of Florence

## What happens

After the death of her father, a great doctor, Helena is living at the Countess of Rousillon's court. She is hopelessly in love with Count Bertram, the countess's son. When Bertram goes to work for the king of France, who is suffering from a terrible illness, Helena follows him. She cures the king using secret medicine recipes left behind by her father. In return, the king says she can choose anyone in his court as her husband – so she chooses Bertram, and they are married.

Unfortunately, Bertram doesn't love Helena. He runs away to fight in a war in Florence in Italy with his best friend Parolles, and sends Helena a letter saying he won't be a true husband to her unless she can take the ring from his finger and bear his child – which, of course, he thinks is impossible. But Helena goes to Florence, where she stays with an old widow. She finds out that Bertram is wooing the widow's daughter, Diana. Helena sends him a false message that she has died, then arranges to take Diana's place in the darkness and spend the night with Bertram. Thinking she is Diana, Bertram gives her his ring. Helena gives him a ring the king had given her.

Eventually, Bertram returns to his mother's house in Rousillon, where the king of France is staying. The king sees the ring he gave to Helena on Bertram's hand, and asks him what is going on. At last, Diana, the widow, and Helena arrive and explain everything. Helena reveals that she has Bertram's ring and is pregnant with his child. Bertram agrees to accept Helena as his wife.

## Famous quotation

*"Love all, trust a few, do wrong to none."*

The countess's advice to Bertram when he leaves home

# Antony and Cleopatra

Type of play: Tragedy
Written: c.1606
In brief: Roman leader Antony shirks his duty to be with Cleopatra, queen of Egypt – leading to bitter war and a tragic ending.

## Main characters

Cleopatra.....................................Queen of Egypt
Antony.........................................Roman general and joint ruler of the Roman empire
Enobarbus...................................Antony's best friend and valued supporter
Octavius Caesar..........................Joint ruler, with Antony and Lepidus, of the Roman empire
Lepidus........................................Joint ruler, with Octavius and Antony, of the Roman empire
Charmian and Iras.......................Cleopatra's loyal ladies-in-waiting

## What happens

Although Antony is one of the three rulers of Rome, he spends most of his time in Egypt, where he is having an affair with the country's glamorous queen, Cleopatra – to the anger of one of his co-rulers, Octavius Caesar. When Antony's wife Fulvia dies, he is forced to return to Rome. There, a rebel leader named Pompey is plotting against the three leaders, and Antony realizes he must stay to defend the city. He also agrees to marry Octavia, Octavius Caesar's sister, as a sign of loyalty to Octavius. When she hears of this marriage, Cleopatra is consumed with jealousy.

The dispute with Pompey is resolved peacefully. But, while Antony and Octavia are away in Athens, Octavius attacks Pompey anyway, and defeats him. He also has Lepidus imprisoned. Antony sends Octavia home to Rome, and heads for Egypt, where he is reunited with Cleopatra. Antony's friend Enobarbus, despairing of his future, deserts him. With the help of the Egyptians, Antony wages war on Octavius, but is defeated. He blames Cleopatra, and she goes into hiding, sending him news that she is dead. On hearing this, Antony is filled with despair. He stabs himself and is taken to Cleopatra, but dies in her arms. Cleopatra, refusing to give herself up to the Romans, has a basket of deadly snakes delivered, and lets one of them bite her. Her servants, Charmian and Iras, die with her.

## Famous quotation

*"Finish, good lady; the bright day is done,
And we are for the dark."*

Cleopatra's servant Iras speaking to her as they prepare to die

# The Comedy of Errors

## Main characters

Type of play: Comedy
Written: c.1592
In brief: After 25 years apart, identical twins and their identical twin servants end up in the same city, leading to comical confusion.

Egeon..........................................An old merchant from Syracuse
Antipholus of Ephesus............................A wealthy merchant of Ephesus
Dromio of Ephesus.................................Bumbling servant of Antipholus of Ephesus
Antipholus of Syracuse.......................... Long-lost twin brother of Antipholus of Ephesus
Dromio of Syracuse................................Bumbling servant of Antipholus of Syracuse
Adriana.................................................Bad-tempered wife of Antipholus of Ephesus
Luciana................................................ Sister of Adriana
Emilia...................................................Abbess of an abbey in Ephesus

## What happens

Egeon, an old man from Syracuse, visits Ephesus. Since the two cities are at war, and citizens are banned from moving between them, Egeon is arrested and taken to be executed. But he pleads with the duke, telling him that he is searching for his family. He explains that he once had identical twin sons – both named Antipholus – but became separated from his wife and one of the twins in a shipwreck 25 years ago. The other twin, Antipholus of Syracuse, has gone looking for his brother and has now disappeared. The duke is sorry for the old man, and agrees to give him one day to find enough money to pay a fine instead of being executed.

As it turns out, Egeon's long-lost son is living in Ephesus, where he is a prosperous merchant. His twin, Antipholus of Syracuse, is also there, having recently arrived, and is searching for his brother. Both twins have servants named Dromio, who are also long-lost identical twins. As the day proceeds, various citizens of Ephesus mistake Antipholus of Syracuse for Antipholus of Ephesus, including his own wife, Adriana. Meanwhile, Antipholus of Syracuse falls in love with Adriana's sister, Luciana. To escape the confusion, Antipholus of Syracuse and his servant end up hiding in the abbey. Finally, everything is sorted out. Emilia, the abbess of the abbey, reveals herself to be Egeon's long-lost wife, and the twins' mother. The twins and their twin servants are reunited with each other, and the play ends with rejoicing.

## Famous quotation

*"There's a time for all things."*

Antipholus of Syracuse, talking to his servant, Dromio

# Coriolanus

## Main characters

Coriolanus (Caius Martius).......................A brave but snobbish Roman general
Volumnia...............................................Coriolanus's bossy mother
Tullus Aufidius.......................................Leader of the Volscians, an enemy tribe
Menenius and Cominius..........................Friends of Coriolanus
Virgilia..................................................Coriolanus's wife
Brutus and Sicinius.................................Roman politicians opposed to Coriolanus

Type of play: Tragedy
Written: c.1607
In brief: Though hailed for his battle victories, Coriolanus offends the people and is thrown out of Rome. His only choice is to team up with his arch enemy.

## What happens

Caius Martius, a brilliant Roman military leader, defeats a tribe named the Volscians, led by his arch enemy, Tullus Aufidius. To mark the victory, Caius Martius is renamed Coriolanus, after the city where the battle took place. Rome's leaders also decide to make him consul (chief magistrate). But before that can happen, Coriolanus upsets the Roman people by seeming to think he is better than them, and refusing to plead for their votes. Two other politicians, Brutus and Sicinius, who do not like Coriolanus, argue that he should not be given any power, and he is eventually driven out of the city.

Coriolanus decides to join forces with his old enemy, Aufidius, in order to attack Rome. Hearing that Coriolanus is leading the Volscians against the city, the Romans panic. When Coriolanus reaches the city gates, his old friends Cominius and Menenius beg him to change his mind, but he refuses. But when his mother, Volumnia, tells him not to attack Rome, he obeys her, and makes a peace pact instead. When he returns to Antium, the Volscians' home ground, the people hail him as a hero. But Aufidius is jealous of his popularity, and calls him a traitor instead. In the argument that follows, Aufidius's men stab Coriolanus to death in front of the crowd.

## Famous quotations

*"I shall be loved when I am lacked."*

Coriolanus speaking to his mother at the gates of Rome

*"Action is eloquence."*

Volumnia, Coriolanus's mother

# Cymbeline

Type of play: Romance
Written: c.1609
In brief: Brave, clever Princess Imogen has a series of adventures before being reunited with her family and her one true love.

## Main characters

Cymbeline...................................King of Britain
Imogen......................................Princess of Britain, Cymbeline's daughter
The Queen.................................The king's evil, cruel wife, and Imogen's stepmother
Posthumus................................An orphan brought up in the king's court, who marries Imogen
Cloten.......................................The Queen's arrogant, foolish son
Iachimo.....................................A scheming Italian gentleman
Belarius.....................................A former nobleman at Cymbeline's court, now living in Wales
Guiderius and Arviragus..............Cymbeline's long-lost sons

## What happens

Princess Imogen secretly marries her friend Posthumus, although she is supposed to marry her stepbrother, Cloten. When the king finds out, he banishes Posthumus to Italy. There, Posthumus meets Iachimo, who makes a bet with Posthumus that Imogen will be unfaithful to him. To win the bet, Iachimo goes to Britain and hides in Imogen's bedroom, then reports details of the bedroom to Posthumus. Posthumus thinks Imogen must have had an affair with Iachimo, and is horrified. He orders a servant to kill her, but instead the servant helps her to escape, disguised as a boy named Fidele.

Imogen goes to Wales and becomes a servant to Belarius, Guiderius and Arviragus. Unbeknown to her or them, Guiderius and Arviragus are really the king's own sons and Imogen's brothers. Belarius kidnapped them and brought them up as his own after being banished from Cymbeline's court. Cloten follows Imogen to Wales, but is killed in a fight with Guiderius and has his head cut off. Imogen takes some medicine given to her by her stepmother the queen, but it turns out to be a poison that sends her into a deep coma. Thinking their servant is dead, Belarius, Guiderius and Arviragus leave Imogen lying alongside Cloten's headless body. When she wakes, she believes it to be Posthumus's body. In despair, she goes to work as a servant for a Roman general who is attacking Britain.

Meanwhile, Posthumus is filled with remorse for ordering Imogen's death. He fights on the British side, but when the Romans are defeated he puts on a Roman uniform and lets himself be taken prisoner, in order to punish himself. Since she's dressed as a Roman servant, Imogen is also taken prisoner, and they both end up at Cymbeline's court. There, the king finally recognizes them and they are reunited. The king is also reunited with his sons, Guiderius and Arviragus, and forgives Belarius for kidnapping them. Posthumus and Imogen forgive Iachimo for his deception. Finally, the evil queen dies, and everyone else lives happily ever after.

# Henry IV (Parts 1 & 2)

Type of play: History
Written: c.1597
In brief: When rebels raise an army against Henry IV, fun-loving Prince Hal proves he's brave enough to become the next king.

## Main characters

Henry IV.................................................. King of England
Prince Henry or "Hal"............................. Henry's high-spirited son
Falstaff.................................................... Hal's friend, an old, fat, drunken nobleman
Poins...................................................... A friend of Hal and Falstaff
Henry Percy or "Hotspur"........................ A bold young rebel soldier
Lord Northumberland.............................. Hotspur's father, who also becomes a rebel
Prince John of Lancaster.......................... Prince Hal's younger brother

## What happens

Shakespeare wrote a set of two plays about Henry IV. In Part 1, Hotspur and his supporters decide to raise a rebel army to overthrow King Henry IV. The king's son, Prince Hal, spends all his time drinking in taverns with his friends Falstaff and Poins. Falstaff carries out a robbery, and Hal and Poins, in disguise, then rob him in turn. Falstaff later boasts about his bravery during the attack, until Hal and Poins reveal that they were the robbers. Then, the king summons Hal to fight in battle against Hotspur. Falstaff turns out to be useless on the battlefield, but Hal fights brilliantly and kills Hotspur. The king makes plans to defeat the remaining rebels.

In Part 2, Lord Northumberland, learning that Hal has killed his son Hotspur, decides to join the other rebels in attacking the king. Meanwhile, Hal has returned to his life of leisure, frequenting taverns and playing tricks on Falstaff. Northumberland changes his mind about fighting the king, and flees to Scotland, but Hal and Falstaff join the army against the other rebels. Hal's brother, Prince John, makes a deal with the rebels; then, when they surrender, they are arrested and sentenced to death. King Henry IV is now dying, and worries that Hal is not mature enough to be king. Hal comes to his bedside and promises he will face up to his responsibilities. The old king dies, and Hal is crowned Henry V. Falstaff comes to greet the new king, but Hal sends him away and tells him not to come back. Now he is king, his days of fun and idleness are over, and he makes plans to invade France.

## Famous quotation

*"Uneasy lies the head that wears a crown."*

King Henry IV, finding it hard to sleep because of his worries about the rebellion

# Henry V

## Main characters

Type of play: History
Written: c.1598
In brief: Henry V makes his mark by invading France. Thanks to his courage and brilliant leadership, the English triumph against all odds.

Henry V (formerly Prince Hal)....................Brave, heroic king of England
Bardolph, Pistol and Nim.........................Old friends of Henry's who join him in battle
Charles VI of France..............................Wise old French king
The Dauphin..........................................French prince and heir to the throne, son of Charles VI
Princess Catherine.................................French princess, daughter of Charles VI

## What happens

Henry V, the new king of England, decides to invade France to claim part of its territory. When he hears this, the arrogant young French prince, known as the Dauphin, sends Henry a mocking, insulting message. But, supported by England's noblemen, clergymen and public, Henry gathers his troops and prepares for battle. Meanwhile, in a tavern in London, the king's former friends Bardolph, Pistol and Nim get ready to leave their families and fight for their country. Their conversation reveals that Falstaff, an old friend whom Henry rejected when he became king, has died.

Henry sets sail for France, after putting to death a trio of spies who are plotting against him. His soldiers conquer the town of Harfleur, and the French king sends a huge army to stop them. The English are outnumbered, but Henry makes a passionate speech to urge them on, and they defeat the French in the Battle of Agincourt. Nim and Bardolph are caught looting (stealing) from the towns they have overthrown, and Henry has them hanged. Finally, the English and the French make a peace deal: Henry gains control over France, and will marry the French king's daughter, Princess Catherine.

## Famous quotation

*"Once more unto the breach, dear friends, once more;*
*Or close the wall up with our English dead...*
*...Follow your spirit, and upon this charge*
*Cry 'God for Harry, England, and Saint George!'"*

The beginning and end of Henry's famous speech urging his men into battle

# Henry VI (Parts 1, 2 & 3)

Type of play: History
Written: c.1590
In brief: Henry VI struggles to control French rebellions and fighting between English lords. Finally, he is overthrown and murdered.

## Main characters

King Henry VI...........................................Weak, timid king of England

Margaret of Anjou....................................Henry's bossy French wife

Lord Talbot..............................................English nobleman and soldier

Joan of Arc..............................................French soldier and battle leader

Richard Plantagenet, Duke of York............Nobleman who rebels against Henry

Edward....................................................Richard of York's eldest son, who eventually becomes king

Richard...................................................Another of Richard of York's sons

## What happens

This is a set of three plays about the reign of Henry VI of England. Part 1 opens with the funeral of the great King Henry V. At first, the new king, Henry's son King Henry VI, is too young to take full control, and various English noblemen struggle for power. Meanwhile, the French rebel against English control, helped by a young female soldier named Joan of Arc. In France, English nobleman Lord Talbot tries to defeat the French rebels. He dies in battle, but finally peace is agreed, Joan of Arc is burned at the stake, and King Henry is engaged to a French noblewoman, Margaret of Anjou.

Unfortunately, Henry's troubles are not over. In Part 2, the English lords continue to quarrel, especially over Henry's marriage agreement, which hands over to France some French land that had previously been ruled by England. In the fighting that follows, two noblemen, Gloucester and Suffolk, end up dead, while the most powerful of the lords, Richard of York, stirs up a rebellion against the king. At the end of the play, Richard fights his main rival, Somerset, and kills him. He now stands ready to try to take control of the country.

In Part 3, Henry resorts to desperate measures. To keep the peace with Richard, he makes him heir to the throne, instead of his own son. But this makes Henry's wife Margaret furious. To get her revenge, she has one of York's sons murdered. Civil war breaks out between York and Henry. York is killed – stabbed to death by Margaret and a nobleman named Clifford. But Henry is taken prisoner, and York's son Edward becomes king. Margaret's army, and various other nobles, try to reclaim the throne for Henry, but in the end, Edward triumphs. Finally, Henry is murdered by Richard, son of Richard of York, and younger brother of Edward. Despite pretending to support his brother Edward, Richard, who is disabled, and bitter about his role in life, secretly wants to be king himself.

# Henry VIII

## Main characters

Type of play: History
Written: c.1612
In brief: At first, Henry VIII lets Cardinal Wolsey tell him what to do. But gradually, he takes back control, and the cardinal faces ruin.

Henry VIII.....................................King of England
Queen Katherine..........................Henry's wife
Cardinal Wolsey...........................A clergyman who has power over the king
Duke of Buckingham...................An innocent nobleman who falls victim to Wolsey's scheming
Anne Bullen..............................A beautiful young woman who becomes Henry's second wife

## What happens

This play was one of the last Shakespeare wrote, and experts think he may have co-written it with another playwright, John Fletcher.

When the play begins, King Henry VIII of England has fallen under the spell of Cardinal Wolsey, a scheming clergyman. Wolsey persuades Henry that a nobleman named Buckingham, who is opposed to Wolsey having so much power, is in fact a traitor. Henry has Buckingham arrested and executed, even though he is actually innocent. Seeing what is going on, the people start to distrust Wolsey and his influence over the king.

Meanwhile, Henry's wife, Queen Katherine, speaks out at a council meeting against the high taxes Wolsey has imposed on the public, and Henry tells Wolsey to cancel them. However, at a party at Wolsey's house, the king meets Anne Bullen, and is amazed by her beauty. He decides he wants to divorce Katherine. He asks the Catholic church in Rome to allow him a divorce, claiming the marriage was never truly legal. Queen Katherine is very upset, as she has been a loyal wife to him for 20 years.

Wolsey wants the divorce to happen too, and tries to persuade Katherine to agree to it. But he doesn't want the king to marry Anne, as he has other plans for him to marry a French woman as part of a treaty with France. He secretly writes to the Pope (the leader of the Catholic church), telling him to refuse to allow Henry a divorce until Anne is out of the picture. When Henry discovers this, he turns against Wolsey and strips him of his power. Even though he has not been granted a divorce, he announces his marriage to Anne, and the people of London flock to see her being crowned queen. Henry and Anne have a daughter, Elizabeth.

# Julius Caesar

## Main characters

Julius Caesar................................Roman military general and politician
Brutus......................................... Roman politician and friend of Julius Caesar
Cassius........................................ A scheming general who plots against Caesar
Casca........................................... A Roman politician who opposes Caesar
Antony......................................... A friend and supporter of Caesar

Type of play: Tragedy
Written: c.1599
In brief: Thinking Caesar wants to seize power in Rome, his friend Brutus has him assassinated. But this only leads to a tragic end for Brutus himself.

## What happens

Julius Caesar has recently returned to Rome after fighting successful battles in Spain, and is popular with the people. But some Roman politicians, including Cassius and Casca, believe he wants too much power. Even though Caesar is modest and refuses to accept a crown, they think he is just pretending in order to hide his ambition from the public. By forging letters from members of the public, Cassius tricks Brutus into believing that the people want Caesar dead. Brutus, Cassius and a group of other politicians call Caesar's friend Antony away, then surround Caesar and stab him to death. After the assassination, Antony pretends to support the killers in order to save his own life; but when he is invited to make a speech to the public, he reveals his true feelings, and turns the crowd against the assassins. The people chase Brutus and Cassius out of Rome, and Antony takes over joint leadership of the city with two other politicians, Octavius and Lepidus.

Brutus and Cassius set up camp outside Rome and prepare to attack the city with their armies. But Brutus is miserable. His wife has killed herself, and he is haunted by the ghost of Caesar. He argues with Cassius, and when they go into battle against Rome's armies, they do badly. Finally, both Cassius and Brutus commit suicide.

## Famous quotations

*"Et tu, Brute?" ("You too, Brutus?")*
Julius Caesar, realizing as he is stabbed that one of the assassins is his old friend Brutus.

*"Friends, Romans, countrymen, lend me your ears."*
Antony speaking to the crowd after Caesar's death

175

# King John

## Main characters

King John................................................ King of England
King Philip............................................... King of France
Arthur.................................................... King John's nephew, the rightful heir to the throne
Constance................................................ Arthur's mother
Hubert................................................... One of King John's men
Prince Henry............................................. King John's son

Type of play: History
Written: c.1596
In brief: The King of France tries to force King John to hand over power to his nephew, Arthur. War follows, and both John and Arthur end up dead.

## What happens

King Philip of France sends a message to King John to say that he should hand the throne over to Arthur, John's young nephew, who is the rightful king. John refuses, and war soon breaks out between England and France. The French decide to attack Angers, a town in France which is ruled by England. But the citizens of Angers have a better idea. They suggest that Philip's son Louis and John's niece Blanche should get married, securing peace between the two countries. Philip and John agree.

Constance, Arthur's mother, is furious with King Philip because he no longer supports Arthur's claim to the throne. Then, John is excommunicated (thrown out of the Catholic church) for disobeying the Pope. Philip is told that unless he wants the same to happen to him, he must become John's enemy. He hesitates but soon gives in, and the war starts again.

This time, John's forces manage to capture Arthur. John asks one of his men, Hubert, to "look after" Arthur, but secretly tells him to kill him. However, Arthur is so sweet and innocent that Hubert cannot bear to kill him. He lets him go, but Arthur dies falling from a castle wall as he runs away. John's noblemen believe John and Hubert are responsible for his death. They are so angry that they desert John and go to fight on the French side. Meanwhile, John eventually makes peace with the Pope, but is poisoned by a monk in a monastery where he is staying. Surrounded by his followers and his son, Prince Henry, John dies from the poison. Henry is declared the new king, and the French offer to end the war.

## Famous quotation

*"Grief fills the room up of my absent child..."*
Constance, weeping after Arthur is taken prisoner

# King Lear

## Main characters

Type of play: Tragedy
Written: c.1605
In brief: Grumpy old King Lear can't tell the difference between true love and false flattery – and pays a terrible price.

King Lear.................................. Old, bad-tempered king of ancient Britain
Cordelia...................................... Lear's gentle, loving youngest daughter
Goneril and Regan...................... Lear's evil, scheming older daughters
Earl of Gloucester...................... Lear's loyal friend
Edmund..................................... Gloucester's bitter and twisted illegitimate son
Edgar......................................... Gloucester's good-hearted other son
Lear's fool................................. Court jester who entertains King Lear

## What happens

King Lear decides to divide his kingdom between his three daughters according to how much they love him. Goneril and Regan make showy displays of love, winning large areas of land. But Cordelia refuses to do the same, although she loves her father, and Lear banishes her. He goes to stay first with Goneril and then with Regan, but since they don't really love him, they soon tire of him, throw him out and plot to kill him. He goes insane and ends up wandering the moors in a storm with his fool.

Meanwhile, Gloucester's illegitimate son Edmund turns Gloucester against his other son, Edgar, to get his inheritance. Edgar flees, while Edmund has affairs with Goneril and Regan. They accuse Gloucester of supporting the king of France, Cordelia's new husband, who wants to help Lear. Regan's husband, the duke of Cornwall, gouges Gloucester's eyes out as a punishment. Edgar, disguised as a beggar, cares for his father. Later, in a fit of jealousy over Edmund, Goneril poisons Regan and then kills herself.

Cordelia and her husband come to Dover with an army to rescue Lear, but they are defeated by forces led by Edmund. Lear and Cordelia are captured and Cordelia is hanged. Lear, realizing Cordelia really loved him, dies of grief. Finally, Edgar kills Edmund and is asked to become the new king.

## Famous quotations

*"How sharper than a serpent's tooth it is,
To have a thankless child!"*

Lear, complaining about Goneril

*"Out, vile jelly!"*

Cornwall, as he gouges out Gloucester's eye

# Love's Labour's Lost

Type of play: Comedy
Written: c.1594
In brief: Just as the King of Navarre and his three courtiers swear to give up on love, four beautiful ladies come to stay...

## Main characters

King Ferdinand...........................................King of Navarre, a kingdom near Spain
Longaville, Maine and Berowne.................The king's noble courtiers
Princess of France.................................. The beautiful daughter of the king of France
Armado..................................................A Spaniard who is visiting King Ferdinand's court
Jacquenetta............................................A local country girl

## What happens

The King of Navarre and his three courtiers, Longaville, Maine and Berowne, swear that they will devote themselves to studying for three years, and will avoid women. Just then, the princess of France arrives to visit, with three ladies-in-waiting. The king is too polite to turn them away, but because of his oath he cannot let them stay in his castle. Instead, they stay in a camp in the castle grounds. Before long, the king has fallen in love with the princess, while his courtiers fall in love with her ladies. Since they are supposed to be ignoring women, all four men try to keep their feelings a secret from each other.

Meanwhile, another visitor, named Armado, has fallen in love with a local girl named Jacquenetta. Soon enough, the king realizes he is not the only one to be in love, and everyone's secrets are revealed. Berowne suggests that they abandon their previous plan, and study love instead. But, just as they are celebrating this decision, news arrives from France that the princess's father has died, and she is now the queen of France. She has to go home to mourn her father and be crowned, and she and her ladies leave, saying they can all meet up again in a year's time.

## Famous quotation

*"At Christmas I no more desire a rose
Than wish a snow in May's new-fangled mirth;
But like of each thing that in season grows."*

Berowne, talking to the king

# Measure for Measure

Type of play: Problem play
Written: c.1604
In brief: When he is given power, Angelo is cruel and unfair. But with some cunning trickery, he is eventually caught.

## Main characters

Vincentio..................................... The wise old duke of Vienna
Angelo........................................ Hard-hearted temporary ruler of Vienna
Claudio.......................................A young man
Isabella....................................... Claudio's sister, who is about to become a nun

## What happens

The duke of Vienna says that for 14 years he has let law and order slip, and the city is becoming immoral. He appoints his deputy, Angelo, to rule for a while, hoping he will crack down on crime. Angelo does so immediately: he sentences a young man, Claudio, to death because his girlfriend, Juliet, is pregnant, and they are not married. An old judge named Escalus objects, saying the sentence is too harsh, but Claudio is thrown into prison to await execution.

Claudio's sister, Isabella, pleads with Angelo to spare her brother's life. Angelo says he will spare Claudio if Isabella sleeps with him. Isabella, who is about to become a nun, is shocked and refuses. She tells Claudio she can do nothing to help him. Then an old friar – who is really Duke Vincentio in disguise – comes to the rescue. Angelo has a fiancée, Mariana, whom he has abandoned, but who still loves him. The friar arranges for Mariana to visit Angelo in the night and pretend to be Isabella. Angelo is convinced it is Isabella, but he breaks his promise anyway, and sends Claudio to be beheaded. Helped by the disguised duke, the jailers save Claudio's life. They show Angelo the head of another prisoner who has already died, saying it is Claudio's.

Finally, the "friar" reveals that he is really the duke, and that he knows what has been going on. Angelo is ordered to marry Mariana, his fiancée, but is then sentenced to death for his cruelty, just as he had sentenced Claudio. However, Mariana and Isabella ask for mercy for him, and he is forgiven. Claudio and Juliet prepare to marry too, and the duke asks Isabella to marry him.

## Famous quotation

*"O, it is excellent*
*To have a giant's strength; but it is tyrannous*
*To use it like a giant."*

Isabella, speaking angrily to Angelo

179

# The Merry Wives of Windsor

Type of play: Comedy
Written: c.1600
In brief: Falstaff tries to persuade two women at once to fall in love with him. But they're smarter than he thinks and the joke's on him.

## Main characters

Falstaff.................................................. A fat old nobleman
Mrs. Ford and Mrs. Page.......................... Respectable ladies
Mr. Ford and Mr. Page............................. Their husbands
Nym and Pistol..................................... Former friends of Falstaff
Anne Page............................................. Mrs. Page's beautiful daughter
Fenton................................................. The man Anne loves

## What happens

This play features Falstaff, a fat, drunken, comic character who also appears in Shakespeare's *Henry IV* history plays. Falstaff is trying to woo two married women, Mrs. Ford and Mrs. Page, for their money. Behind Falstaff's back, two of his old friends, Nym and Pistol, tell the women's husbands what he is doing.

Falstaff sends love letters to both women, but they compare the letters and realize they are from the same person. They decide to trick Falstaff, and invite him to Mrs. Ford's house. Saying they must hide him from Mr. Ford, they have Falstaff carried out of the house in a basket of smelly laundry. Later, they play the same trick again, but disguise Falstaff as an old lady before having him chased out of the house. Finally, the women and their husbands fool Falstaff a third time by arranging for him to meet Mrs. Ford in some haunted woods. While there, he is "haunted" and terrified by the Fords' friends and children dressed up as ghosts and fairies.

Meanwhile, three suitors are competing to marry Anne, Mrs. Page's daughter. She prefers a poor man named Fenton, but her parents prefer the other two suitors. During the confusion in the woods, the other two suitors are tricked, while Anne marries Fenton.

## Famous quotation

*"Why, then the world's mine oyster,
Which I with sword will open."*

Pistol speaking to Falstaff, using a phrase which has now become part of modern English

180

# Much Ado About Nothing

Type of play: Problem play
Written: c.1598
In brief: When Don Pedro visits Leonato, two new love affairs begin – but evil, trickery and pride get in the way.

## Main characters

Don Pedro.................................................. Prince of Aragon
Leonato..................................................... Rich, kind old nobleman
Claudio.................................................... A romantic young soldier
Hero........................................................ Leonato's sweet, beautiful daughter
Beatrice................................................... Leonato's witty, sharp-tongued niece
Benedick.................................................. A bold, witty soldier
Don John.................................................. Don Pedro's bitter, evil brother
Dogberry................................................. A comic local police constable

## What happens

After a recent war, Don Pedro comes to stay at Leonato's house with his soldiers, who include Benedick, Claudio, and Don John, Don Pedro's brother. Claudio falls in love with Leonato's pretty daughter Hero, while Benedick has lots of arguments with Leonato's niece, Beatrice. Everyone thinks they are falling in love too, but they swear they are not.

Don Pedro arranges for Claudio to marry Hero, but then the evil Don John tricks Claudio into thinking that Hero has been unfaithful to him. On the wedding day, Claudio wrongly accuses Hero of betraying him. She is so upset that she faints and appears to be dead. Benedick blames Claudio and challenges him to a duel. But then Dogberry and his assistant discover that it's Don John who is really to blame, and that Hero was innocent.

Claudio, believing Hero to be dead, is filled with remorse. He says he will do anything to make amends, so when he is asked to marry a cousin of Hero's whom he has never met, he agrees. At the wedding, she turns out to be Hero, recovered from her coma. Meanwhile, various friends of Beatrice and Benedick trick them into revealing their love for each other, and they agree to marry as well. The play ends with celebrations and dancing.

## Famous quotation

*"I had rather hear my dog bark at a crow than a man swear he loves me."*

*Beatrice, claiming she's not interested in love*

# Othello

Type of play: Tragedy
Written: c.1604
In brief: When Othello marries Desdemona, his so-called friend Iago tricks him into thinking she's a cheat - with tragic results.

## Main characters

Othello........................... A black military general in Venice
Brabantio...................... A Venetian politician
Desdemona.................... Othello's wife, and daughter of Brabantio
Cassio........................... Othello's lieutenant (second-in-command)
Iago.............................. Othello's ensign (third-in-command)
Emilia........................... Iago's wife, and Desdemona's lady-in-waiting

## What happens

Against her father's wishes, Desdemona, the daughter of Brabantio, secretly marries Othello. Although Brabantio is angry, Othello argues that he is worthy of her. He then sets sail for the island of Cyprus to defend it against an attack. Othello's ensign, Iago, is jealous of Cassio, who has a higher rank than him in Othello's army. So Iago turns Othello against Cassio by getting Cassio drunk and involving him in a fight. Othello punishes Cassio by giving him a lower rank.

Cassio asks Desdemona to beg Othello to forgive him, and she goes to Othello to plead with him on Cassio's behalf. Iago suggests to Othello that Desdemona and Cassio are in love with each other, although this is not true. Then, through his wife Emilia, who is Desdemona's lady-in-waiting, Iago steals one of Desdemona's handkerchiefs and plants it on Cassio. Convinced of her infidelity, and driven insane with jealously, Othello kills his wife. Too late, Emilia explains what has happened, and Othello commits suicide.

## Famous quotations

*"O, beware, my lord, of jealousy!*
*It is the green-eyed monster..."*

Iago pretending to warn Othello against jealousy, while tricking him into being jealous

*"One that loved not wisely*
*but too well."*

Othello describing himself at the end of the play

# Pericles

Type of play: Romance
Written: c.1608
In brief: On his travels,
Pericles finds a wife
and has a daughter,
but loses them. 16
years pass before
they can be reunited.

## Main characters

Pericles.......................................Prince of Tyre
King of Antioch...........................A wicked king who wants Pericles dead
Cleon..........................................King of Tarsus
Dionyza.......................................Cleon's wife
Simonides...................................King of Pentapolis
Thaisa.........................................Princess of Pentapolis, who becomes Pericles's wife
Marina.........................................Daughter of Pericles and Thaisa
Lysimachus.................................Ruler of Mytilene

## What happens

Pericles, prince of Tyre, is on the run from the king of Antioch, who is angry because Pericles knows secrets about his wicked crimes. On his travels, Pericles makes friends with Cleon, king of Tarsus, and his wife Dionyza. Later, Pericles is shipwrecked and washed ashore in the land of Pentapolis. He hears that Simonides, king of Pentapolis, is holding a jousting contest the next day, and that the winner will be allowed to marry his beautiful daughter, Thaisa. Pericles enters the contest, wins, and marries Thaisa.

Then Pericles hears that the evil king of Antioch has died, and he can go home. He sets sail with his new wife. On the journey, Thaisa gives birth to a baby girl, named Marina, but dies in childbirth. She is buried at sea in a sealed wooden chest. Unbeknown to Pericles, the chest is washed ashore at Ephesus, where a doctor manages to revive Thaisa, who was not really dead after all. Pericles fears his baby daughter Marina will not survive the rest of the sea journey, so he stops off at Tarsus and leaves her with Cleon and Dionyza, asking them to bring her up. Back in Tyre, Pericles becomes king.

Meanwhile, Marina grows up to be so kind and beautiful that Dionyza grows jealous for her own daughter, and plans to have Marina murdered. Marina escapes, but is captured by pirates and ends up working as a singer in another city, Mytilene, where she is famed for her sweet, kind nature. When she is 16, Pericles sails to Tarsus to visit her, and Cleon and Dionyza tell him she has died. Struck dumb with grief, Pericles stops at Mytilene, and the governor, Lysimachus, sends Marina to try to cheer him up. Talking to her, Pericles realizes she is his long-lost daughter. Lysimachus and Marina arrange to marry. Finally, in a dream, the goddess Diana tells Pericles to visit Ephesus. There, Pericles and Marina find Thaisa alive, and the whole family is reunited.

# Richard II

## Main characters

Richard II.................................King of England
Henry Bolingbroke.......................Richard's cousin
John of Gaunt............................Bolingbroke's father and Richard's uncle

Type of play: History
Written: c.1595
In brief: Richard II is a
weak king who doesn't
know how to run a
country or manage
his money. Before
long, he's in trouble...

## What happens

King Richard II banishes his cousin Bolingbroke and another man, Thomas Mowbray, for arguing. This upsets Bolingbroke's aged father, John of Gaunt. Richard decides to raise money to fight a rebellion in Ireland. John of Gaunt warns him not to waste money in this way, but Richard ignores him, and when John dies, confiscates his wealth. Many noblemen are angry about this, and decide to support Bolingbroke as king. Bolingbroke returns from abroad and Richard is forced to surrender the crown. He is sent to Pomfret Castle, and killed by one of Bolingbroke's supporters.

# Richard III

## Main characters

Richard III..............................King of England
Edward and George........................Richard's brothers
Duke of Buckingham.......................Supporter of Richard
Henry Tudor, Earl of Richmond............Enemy of Richard

Type of play: History
Written: c.1592
In brief: Bitter and
twisted Richard
murders his way to the
throne – but despite his
evil ways, he can't hold
onto power for long.

## What happens

At the start of the play, Richard's brother Edward IV is king. Richard tells him that their brother George is plotting against him, so Edward has George killed. Then Edward dies too. Richard imprisons Edward's two young sons in the Tower of London. He promises to make the duke of Buckingham an earl, and in return Buckingham helps Richard to become king. Then Richard murders Edward's two sons, and refuses to give Buckingham his earldom. Buckingham joins Richard's enemies, but is captured and killed. Finally, Henry Tudor, earl of Richmond, raises an army to fight Richard. Their forces meet at Bosworth. The night before the battle, the ghosts of Richard's victims torment him, while urging Henry Tudor on. The next day, Henry wins the battle, kills Richard, and becomes King Henry VII.

# Timon of Athens

## Main characters

Timon...........................................A nobleman of Athens
Flavius........................................ Timon's loyal servant
Alcibiades..................................An Athenian soldier and friend of Timon
Apemantus................................An Athenian who is scornful of Timon and his friends

Type of play: Tragedy
Written: c.1607
In brief: Wealthy Timon bankrupts himself by being too generous, then finds his old friends won't help him. He turns his back on the world, and dies angry and alone.

## What happens

Nobleman Timon is extremely generous, providing endless gifts and feasts for all his friends. But one day his servant Flavius tells Timon he is badly in debt, and that the people who have lent him money want to be paid back. Timon sends other servants out to his friends' houses to ask them to help him by lending him more money. But despite Timon's previous generosity to them, they all refuse. Timon is furious at his friends' attitudes. In a rage, he invites everyone he knows for one last feast. When the dishes are uncovered, the guests find boiling water and stones instead of food. Having made his point, Timon storms out of Athens and goes to live in the woods.

Meanwhile, another Athenian, Alcibiades, tries to save a friend from being sentenced to death for killing someone in a fight. This annoys the leaders of Athens so much, they banish Alcibiades, and he ends up in the woods, where he finds Timon. Timon has found buried gold there, and gives some to Alcibiades, urging him to attack Athens. Another Athenian, Apemantus, also visits Timon in the woods in order to mock and scorn him. And Flavius goes to the woods too, taking the last of Timon's money to give to him. Timon realizes that Flavius is his only real friend, and gives him some gold.

The leaders of Athens ask Timon to come back, hoping he will be able to stop Alcibiades from attacking the city. Having given up on humanity, Timon refuses, but instead of attacking Athens, Alcibiades strikes a peace deal. He decides to attack only those who have insulted him and Timon. News arrives that Timon has died, and Alcibiades makes a speech about him, praising his good qualities.

# Titus Andronicus

Type of play: Tragedy
Written: c.1593
In brief: Titus and his archenemy Tamora are determined to get their revenge on each other. By the end of the play, hardly anyone is left alive!

## Main characters

Titus Andronicus......................... Roman general
Tamora....................................... Queen of the Goths
Aaron........................................ Tamora's lover
Lavinia...................................... Titus's daughter
Saturnius................................... Emperor of Rome
Lucius....................................... Titus's son

## What happens

After leading his armies in a war against a tribe called the Goths, Titus returns to the city of Rome. He has lost many of his own sons in the battle, but he has captured Tamora, the queen of the Goths, and her sons. Titus sacrifices Tamora's eldest son in retribution for his own sons, and Tamora swears she'll get her revenge. Emperor Saturnius, who had planned to marry Titus's daughter Lavinia, instead decides he likes Tamora, and chooses her as his bride.

This gives Tamora new power, and she and her lover Aaron begin to plot against Titus in order to avenge Tamora's son's death. They frame two of Titus's sons, who end up being beheaded for a murder they didn't commit. Then Tamora tells two of her own sons to attack Titus's daughter Lavinia; they leave her with her hands and tongue cut off. Finally, Titus's last son, Lucius, is banished from Rome and decides to attack the city.

While Lucius manages to capture Aaron, Tamora and her surviving sons disguise themselves and go to visit Titus. But Titus recognizes them. To punish Tamora, he secretly has her sons killed and baked in a pie, which he serves up to Tamora before killing her. The play ends with a bloodbath in which most of the characters, including Titus and Saturnius, are killed. Titus's son Lucius becomes the new emperor of Rome.

## Famous quotation

*"If one good deed in all my life I did,
I do repent it from my very soul."*

Aaron asserting his evil nature

# Troilus and Cressida

## Main characters

Troilus........................................A Trojan prince
Cressida......................................A young Trojan woman
Calchas.......................................Cressida's father, a Trojan priest who has joined the Greeks
Pandarus.....................................Cressida's uncle
Diomedes....................................A Greek soldier
Ulysses.......................................One of the leaders of the Greek army
Hector........................................Troilus's brother and leader of the Trojan forces
Achilles.......................................A Greek leader and great soldier

Type of play: Problem play
Written: c.1601
In brief: Troilus and Cressida fall in love against the backdrop of the Trojan war – but their happiness is to be short-lived.

## What happens

During the 10-year-long Trojan War between the ancient Greeks and the city of Troy, Troilus and Cressida fall in love. Troilus is a Trojan prince, while Cressida is the daughter of a Trojan priest who has changed sides and joined the Greeks. As the war rages in the background, Cressida's uncle Pandarus helps the young lovers and arranges for them to meet up, and they swear everlasting love for each other.

However, Cressida's father, Calchas, arranges for a Trojan prisoner in the Greek camp to be sent back to Troy, and for Cressida to be brought out of Troy in return and delivered to the Greek camp, so that he can be reunited with his daughter. A Greek soldier named Diomedes comes to take Cressida away, and she is separated from Troilus.

During a break in the fighting, Troilus visits the Greek leaders along with his brother Hector. One of the Greeks, Ulysses, shows him to Calchas's tent, where he plans to visit Cressida. But, to his horror, he sees Cressida flirting with Diomedes and agreeing to become his girlfriend. Heartbroken and furious, Troilus returns to the battlefield at his brother's side. The play ends when Hector is killed by the Greeks' best soldier, Achilles.

# The Two Gentlemen of Verona

Type of play: Comedy
Written: c.1594
In brief: Valentine and Proteus are best friends until they both fall for the same woman. But in the end, they are reunited, and each ends up with a wife.

## Main characters

Proteus and Valentine...................Two young friends from Verona
Julia.............................................Girlfriend of Proteus
Silvia...........................................Feisty young lady of Milan
Duke of Milan............................Sylvia's father

## What happens

Valentine sets off to see the world, saying goodbye to his best friend Proteus, who is staying behind in Verona to be with his girlfriend Julia. However, when Valentine has gone, Proteus's father says he is sending him to serve the duke of Milan for a while. Proteus and Julia exchange rings and swear everlasting love, and Proteus goes to Milan. He finds that Valentine is already there, and has fallen in love with the duke's daughter, Silvia. Soon, Proteus falls in love with Silvia too, and plots against Valentine. He tells the duke that Valentine and Silvia are planning to run away together, and Valentine is banished. He becomes the leader of a band of outlaws.

Meanwhile, Julia disguises herself as a pageboy named Sebastian, and goes to Milan to be with Proteus. But when she arrives, to her horror, she sees Proteus and Thurio, a rich, foolish nobleman, both wooing Silvia. Silvia, however, still prefers Valentine, and goes into the forest to look for him. The duke, Proteus, Thurio and "Sebastian" (Julia in disguise) follow Silvia to bring her back.

In the forest, Silvia is surrounded by outlaws and her bodyguard runs away. Proteus rescues her, not realizing that Valentine is watching secretly from among the trees. Proteus thinks Silvia should agree to be his in return for being rescued, but she refuses and he tries to use violence to force her to agree. Valentine jumps out and saves Silvia from Proteus. Seeing his old friend, Proteus is so sorry that he begs forgiveness for his conduct. Valentine forgives Proteus and says he can have Silvia after all, even though this is not what she wants. But just then the others arrive, and "Sebastian" faints. Her real identity as Julia is revealed, and Proteus realizes he loves her after all. Seeing Valentine's brave and kind nature, the duke agrees that he can marry Silvia. Both the weddings are planned for later that day.

## Famous quotation

*"What light is light, if Silvia be not seen?*
*What joy is joy, if Silvia be not by?"*

Valentine, speaking of his love for Silvia

# The Two Noble Kinsmen

## Main characters

Theseus.....................................Duke of Athens
Hippolyta...................................Wife of Theseus
Palamon and Arcite.....................Two noblemen of Thebes
Creon.........................................Duke of Thebes
Emilia........................................Hippolyta's sister

Type of play: Comedy
Written: c.1612
In brief: Palamon and Arcite fall out over Emilia, a woman they hardly know. From then on they are determined to fight a duel over her.

## What happens

Palamon and Arcite are two kinsmen (relatives) of Creon, the duke of Thebes. They are called upon to fight in battle when Theseus, duke of Athens, declares war on Creon. Theseus wins the war, and Palamon and Arcite are taken prisoner. Theseus has their wounds treated, but then puts them in prison. From their cell window, they see the beautiful Emilia, the sister of Theseus's wife Hippolyta, walking in a garden, and both fall in love with her at once. They start arguing over her, and resolve to fight a duel. The jailer separates them and takes Arcite to the duke, who banishes him from Athens. The jailer's daughter falls in love with Palamon and helps him to escape. Both kinsmen end up wandering in the woods outside Athens.

Arcite sees a troop of athletes training to take part in the games to entertain Theseus and Hippolyta. He disguises himself and joins them. In the games, he does so well that Theseus, Hippolyta and Emilia reward him and he becomes popular at their court. Later, on a visit to the woods, Arcite finds Palamon, weary and hungry. They decide they will still fight their duel over Emilia. Arcite brings Palamon food to revive him, and they are about to start fighting when Theseus's men catch them. They explain that they both love Emilia, so Theseus asks Emilia to choose between them, but she cannot. Eventually, Theseus orders a contest of strength between the men: the winner will marry Emilia, and the loser will be put to death. The contest is held and Arcite wins. Palamon is about to be executed when news arrives that Arcite has fallen off his horse and been fatally wounded. The two kinsmen make friends again, Arcite dies and Palamon is allowed to marry Emilia.

# Shakespeare's poetry

## Poems and patrons

In Shakespeare's time, writing plays for the theatre was a good way of making money, but – then as now – it was harder to make a living from poetry. Poets usually had rich patrons who would give them money. In return, poets would write poems about their patrons, or dedicate their poetry to them. One of Shakespeare's patrons was an earl named Henry Wriothesley. Shakespeare wrote several long poems, such as *Venus and Adonis*, for him. Other poems by Shakespeare include *The Phoenix and the Turtle* and *The Lover's Complaint*.

## The sonnets

A sonnet is a short poem with 14 lines and a strict rhyme scheme. In the early 1600s, Shakespeare wrote a famous set of 154 sonnets, which have become his most popular poems. They are mainly about love, but they are quite mysterious as it's not clear who they are addressed to. It could be one of Shakespeare's patrons, but no one knows for sure.

Shakespeare's sonnets are famous for their beautiful descriptions and images of nature. They describe trees, flowers, birdsong, the seashore, the weather and the seasons in their attempts to evoke the experience of being in love. The sonnet below, number 18 in the sequence, is one of the most famous of all:

> Shall I compare thee to a summer's day?
> Thou art more lovely and more temperate:
> Rough winds do shake the darling buds of May,
> And summer's lease hath all too short a date:
> Sometime too hot the eye of heaven shines,
> And often is his gold complexion dimm'd;
> And every fair from fair sometime declines,
> By chance or nature's changing course untrimm'd;
> But thy eternal summer shall not fade
> Nor lose possession of that fair thou owest;
> Nor shall Death brag thou wander'st in his shade,
> When in eternal lines to time thou growest:
> So long as men can breathe or eyes can see,
> So long lives this, and this gives life to thee.

# Index of plays and tales

This book includes all Shakespeare's plays, either retold as tales, or as plot summaries at the back of the book. You can use this at-a-glance index to find the one you want quickly.